THRIVE

THRIVE

How the Science of the
Adolescent Brain Helps Us Imagine a
Better Future for All Children

LISA M. LAWSON

With a foreword by
Governor Wes Moore

NEW YORK
LONDON

© 2025 by Lisa M. Lawson
Foreword © 2025 by Wes Moore
All rights reserved.
No part of this book may be reproduced, in any form, without written permission from the publisher.

Requests for permission to reproduce selections from this book should be made through our website: https://thenewpress.org/contact-us/.

Published in the United States by The New Press, New York, 2025
Distributed by Two Rivers Distribution

ISBN 978-1-62097-969-3 (hc)
ISBN 978-1-62097-998-3 (ebook)
CIP data is available

The New Press publishes books that promote and enrich public discussion and understanding of the issues vital to our democracy and to a more equitable world. These books are made possible by the enthusiasm of our readers; the support of a committed group of donors, large and small; the collaboration of our many partners in the independent media and the not-for-profit sector; booksellers, who often hand-sell New Press books; librarians; and above all by our authors.

www.thenewpress.com

Composition by Dix Digital Prepress and Design
This book was set in Adobe Garamond and Janson Text

Printed in the United States of America

10 9 8 7 6 5 4 3 2 1

For my father, who gave me roots and wings.

"It is easier to build strong children than to repair broken men."

Frederick Douglass

Contents

Foreword — *xi*
Introduction — *xvii*

Part I: The Adolescent Brain
   1. The Adolescent Brain — 3
   2. Challenges Adolescents Face — 15
   3. A New Approach — 31

Part II: The Components of a Healthy Adolescence
   4. Basic Needs — 41
   5. Permanent Connections — 59
   6. Education and Credentials — 77
   7. Financial Stability and Well-Being — 89
   8. Youth Leadership: Taking Charge of Their Lives — 105

Part III: A Call to Action to Thrive
   9. The Ecosystem It Takes to Thrive — 119
   10. Public Systems and Policymakers — 135
   11. Employers — 151
   12. The Social Sector — 165
   13. Coordination and Navigation — 175

Conclusion — *187*
Acknowledgments — *193*
Notes — *197*
Index — *211*

Foreword

During my first four days of military school, I tried to run away five times. I would lay in bed with my eyes closed and wait for the other cadets to fall asleep. Then, I'd climb out of my bunk and run into the woods. Getting lost didn't take long. After thirty minutes of wandering through the school grounds, I would get caught and be brought back to my bed. Other students started giving me hand-drawn maps with instructions on how to break free from our campus and get safely to a neighboring town. The landmarks on the map were made up and the directions led nowhere.

My mother saw military school as a last resort in response to a seemingly endless chain of misbehavior at home. My teachers placed me on disciplinary and academic probation before I hit double digits. At age eleven, I felt handcuffs on my wrists. Mom started leaving brochures on the kitchen table featuring glossy images of teenagers in flat-brim hats and gray uniforms bearing military insignia on their shoulders. I thought it was all one big, drawn-out joke. But my mom was dead serious. A few weeks before my thirteenth birthday, I started school at Valley Forge Military Academy in Delaware County, Pennsylvania.

After my fifth failed attempt at running away, I called Mom and begged her to take me home. Gripping the phone and holding back tears, I rattled off whatever I thought she wanted to hear from me.

"I love you so much."

"I promise I will be better."

"You were right and I was wrong."

But nothing was going to change her mind.

Foreword

Mom spoke slowly but clearly from the other end of the line. "Wes, too many people have fought and saved and prayed for you to go to that school," she said. "You have a big team rooting for you. We love you, and we will not allow you to throw away your potential."

Click.

The decision was final. I would stay at Valley Forge.

I wish I could say that everything suddenly turned around in my life, that a heavenly light shined down on me and illuminated a path to success. In reality, I was just plain angry at my mom. I stayed angry with her for a long time. I kept getting in trouble at school and kept trying to escape. But time wore down my stubbornness. And slowly, things changed. On those occasions when I would actually listen to my teachers, I heard them talk about words like honor, code, and service. After being assigned a few marginal leadership positions in my class in order to teach me responsibility, I learned what it meant to be accountable for the person to my left and my right. I started to take a real interest in campus life and academics. By senior year, I had risen to the rank of captain, commanding around 800 cadets. And after graduating from high school at Valley Forge, I decided I wanted to stay for a few more years. I enrolled in the junior college on campus, received my associate's degree, and completed the U.S. Army's Early Commissioning Program. I was so young that my mom had to sign my military paperwork.

I walked onto the Valley Forge campus as a twelve-year-old boy with a complicated past and a questionable future. I walked off the Valley Forge campus as a young man who'd earned the respect of his peers and felt deeply prepared to lead and to serve. After graduation, I studied at Johns Hopkins and Oxford, deployed to Afghanistan with the 82nd Airborne Division, ran one of the largest poverty-fighting organizations in the country, and now, I serve as the 63rd governor of Maryland and the first Black governor in the history of my state.

Foreword

My story underscores the pivotal role that adolescence plays in the development of motivation, personality, character, empathy, focus, and drive. Popular wisdom dictates that rapid brain development takes place only in children under the age of five. But what my experience demonstrates—and what emerging discoveries in the field of brain science strongly suggest—is that we each continue to undergo profound personal, emotional, and neurological development deep into adolescence and young adulthood. And my journey is proof. Of course, I don't mean to suggest that every parent should send their child to military school. But if we want to build avenues to success for more Americans, we need to ensure the road to opportunity doesn't stop short once you turn six.

Under the leadership of president and CEO Lisa Lawson, the Annie E. Casey Foundation has been leading the charge to ensure that all young people—especially those who face the steepest barriers—can realize their God-given potential well into adulthood. Lawson's approach is guided by a renewed focus on adolescents and young people in their early twenties. This stage in development and growth sets the stage for everything else that will follow, from educational attainment to job opportunities to financial security. Lawson calls on us to focus more intently on this critical period of life, and she has laid out five clear priority areas to scaffold that vision: basic needs; permanent connections; education and credentials; financial stability; and leadership opportunities. This book explores each of these areas in detail, providing a road map for how we can build more pathways to prosperity and leave no one behind.

In the pages that follow, Lawson has compiled a trove of cutting-edge brain science in order to shine a light on why we, as citizens and leaders, need to widen our understanding of human flourishing. She lays out the stages of adolescence, the positive and negative experiences that affect brain development, and the personal and institutional supports that can ensure all young people more easily thrive. Most importantly, this book serves as a call to action for public systems, policymakers, the social sector, businesses, and communities. As Lawson argues throughout this groundbreaking exploration of opportunity and action, the time is *now* for us to rally around our youth and equip them with the fundamental supports they need to transition successfully into adulthood—from education to employment.

For Lawson, these topics are more than talking points; they are deeply personal. I know because I've had the privilege of working alongside her for years. We met through my mother, who was hired by the Annie E. Casey Foundation when I was fourteen years old. That first position at Casey didn't just change my mother's life, it provided enough money and strong enough benefits to change the trajectory of our entire family. Throughout my childhood, Mom had to juggle multiple jobs to support me and my two sisters. After she got hired by Casey, she only had to work one job.

A few years ago, my mom introduced me to Lisa, who joined Casey after a fourteen-year career with UPS. I could immediately sense her passion for the issues she works on every day, guided by a profound love of family. In every child, Lisa sees her own daughter and wants to help all our young people navigate the rocky transition from home life into the real world.

As president of the Casey Foundation, Lisa Lawson has built on the organization's decades-long tradition of elevating our youth by applying her vast wealth of professional knowledge and personal wisdom, honed over a distinguished career in philanthropy. Lisa believes that we are stronger together, and her leadership has focused on how we build new partnerships across the public, private, philanthropic, and nonprofit sectors in order to deliver results. One of her first priorities as CEO of Casey was to launch Thrive by 25®, a program that aims to improve the well-being of youth and young adults from ages fourteen to twenty-four. This initiative is guided by a spirit of innovation and partnership and has already helped transform the contemporary landscape of how we support kids and families in America.

In Maryland, we are proud to call the Annie E. Casey Foundation one of our own. Casey has been a cornerstone of Maryland pride since it moved to Baltimore in 1994. And in the halls of the Annapolis State House, my administration has partnered with Lisa and the Annie E. Casey Foundation to craft, refine, and launch a number of key initiatives intended to support our children and youth. At the heart of our partnership is a shared commitment to innovation.

Together, we are bringing everyone to the table to build new pathways to work, wages, and wealth for our youth. And that cause has never been more important. We live in a moment of profound uncertainty, where our young people feel increasingly isolated and unmoored. Cycles of poverty and tragedy have gone unaddressed for far too long. The public is tired of hearing the same solutions to the same problems and being asked to expect different results. With this as our context, we must join hands across all corners of society and prioritize the enactment of new, creative strategies to uplift our young people and demonstrate to our children that there is more to life than what is directly in front of them. Our children are our future, and they deserve nothing less than our full support.

But change cannot be guided by blind hope—it must be rooted in data and fact. That is what this book provides. By studying Lawson's research and analysis, we can better grasp what happens inside the brains of adolescents and more clearly understand what they need from the adults in their lives. Only with that knowledge at our fingertips can we truly enact effective, society-wide changes to help our most vulnerable communities thrive. In addition to the research and analyses included in this book, Lawson has laid out clear, actionable steps that governments, lawmakers, businesses, communities, philanthropic organizations, and households can take to help our children get ahead in life. These policy prescriptions will help lay the foundation for progress in community centers and legislative chambers across the country for years to come.

There's an African proverb that states, "If you want to go fast, go alone. If you want to go far, go together." Lisa Lawson calls on us to go fast, go far, and go together. It is a mindset that often gets endorsed but rarely enacted. When I spoke to my mom that night from Valley Forge thirty years ago, she reminded me about all the people who were a part of my story, pulling me out of the difficulties of my childhood and toward a brighter future. I didn't realize it then, but I was standing on the shoulders of family members, friends, loved ones, and total strangers who lifted me up until I was strong enough to make it on my own two feet. No child finds fulfillment on their own. Our children's successes are the product of the entire village, working together to realize the immense aspirations we hold for the next generation. That message is at the heart of this book. Lisa Lawson bravely calls upon all of us to do our part in order to ensure that young people have the tools they need to build lives of happiness, joy, and wealth. And if we heed her call and closely study her words, I believe we can build the kind of society that those who came before us fought for, and one that those who come after us deserve.

Governor Wes Moore
Baltimore, Maryland
December 2024

Introduction

I love teenagers.

That might surprise you, as popular culture paints teenagers in a negative light more often than it celebrates them. But there is so much for us to love—and learn—about this in-between time beyond outdated stereotypes.

My love for teenagers started well before I had one of my own, and in an unexpected way. I had worked for years at law firms and shipping giant UPS—both in business roles and its philanthropic arm, the UPS Foundation. Then I decided to fully dive into philanthropy because I felt called to use my skills to invest in programs and people working to improve the lives of others. UPS founder Jim Casey and his three siblings created the Annie E. Casey Foundation to honor the strength of their widowed mother in keeping the family together through hard times. The mission of the Foundation they named after her aligned with my values—to strengthen families and communities and ensure access to opportunity for children, youth, and young adults.

I joined the Foundation when my daughter was nine. Like me, she would grow up an only child; like me, I wanted her to have a childhood of deep nurturing, attention, support, and inspiration.

I grew up in Atlanta, Georgia, and was surrounded by aunts, uncles, and grandparents. My family had high expectations for themselves, and for me. My parents never moved from the home and community I was born into. It would be different for my daughter. She was born in Atlanta, but we relocated to Baltimore,

Introduction

the headquarters of the Foundation. I wondered how I might create a village of support for my daughter away from the only source of familial strength we'd known.

Years later, a little nervous about what changes the teen years would bring, I found myself eager for guidance on how to parent my daughter as she grew older. At the time, I was traveling around the country, meeting and talking with hundreds of young people, community leaders, and service providers as part of my work. These conversations eventually planted the seeds for this book.

In 2016, I attended a conference in St. Louis with my Foundation colleagues. We spent several days together reflecting on our work strengthening and supporting children and families. We focused on how teenagers and young adults in foster care and the juvenile justice system might come through those challenging experiences differently and be ready for adulthood—and we explored how adults could best support these young people.

That day, we also heard from a group of people who were at the heart of our work but didn't always have a voice in the room when we made decisions that affected their lives: teenagers.

The Foundation had worked with this group of teens for many months, helping them understand that the physical and emotional changes happening inside their bodies were part of a bigger, more complex system of changes involving their brains. This process ultimately informed a set of tools, called *Brain Frames*, that Casey developed to help adults better understand and support young people in foster care. This effort went way beyond a typical adolescent lesson on the basics of puberty and safe sex. It unlocked the science behind the behavior of teens that adults often find so perplexing, with the goal of serving them better and in ways that truly align with their development process.

I sat rapt as the young presenters taught me something essential about the key challenge facing all adolescents. Teens crave thrilling new experiences and place immense value on the opinions of their peer group because their brains are still developing—and the parts of the brain that control those things are highly active.

The teen brain that starts skateboarding—as a new, thrilling, risk-taking experience—is the same teen brain that chooses to steal a car. Both teen brains are eager to take a risk and impress their friends, even if the adults in their lives disapprove of their choices. How teens choose to express their need for risk-taking and peer validation during this window of their lives—and how we shape or respond to those choices—could make or break the rest of their lives.

The conference presentation was the first time I would see the people directly affected by policy talking to people in power about what they needed. In this case, there was a twist—these were teenagers who were not yet old enough to enlist in the military, to vote, or to have passed through other rites that our society deems as markers of maturity, but their experiences were powerful. And they showed that they were capable of interpreting and understanding these experiences, too.

I listened intently as one of the teenagers who had learned about the adolescent brain launched into a direct and clear explanation of how their brain develops. Using their hand clasped in a fist, I watched as they pointed to different parts of their hand and explained brain development as something that happens from the back of the organ to the front. They sounded confident and calm as they used specific medical terms to describe the front of the brain, the prefrontal cortex, and how it develops over time and does not complete its growth until about age twenty-five. This critical area, the teen explained, shapes memory, flexible thinking, organization, attention, and emotional regulation.

That science was completely new to me, and it sparked something meaningful in both my heart and mind. I couldn't have known it then, but that presentation was the beginning of a fundamental shift in how I would see teenagers. They weren't just little adults; they were distinct, still-developing people filled with possibility, opportunity, and hope. These teens were in a physically and emotionally dynamic period in human life—just like babies and toddlers—with tremendous potential to unleash.

From that day on, I started to dig deeper into what I learned, and I came to know that adolescent brain science and development, according to the National Academies of Sciences, begins with the onset of puberty and ends in the mid-twenties. As I kept learning on my own, I had an experience that I can only describe as falling in love with the promise that lies within each adolescent and the transformative opportunity we as adults have to shape their journey. And like any person in love, my adoration for young people made me approach everything about my life, personally and professionally, dramatically differently.

At Casey, I moved up the ranks to eventually become president and CEO. As I did, I held on to that day in St. Louis. I pushed to embed an understanding of adolescent brain science into all aspects of our work as an essential strategy to help guide young people successfully into adulthood.

It has become obvious to me that so much of the way we serve and interact with young people is based on fears for their physical and emotional safety, like being tempted by drug use or becoming a teen parent. I have to admit that I had similar fears as my daughter approached her teen years.

Although the nonprofit field has been moving in the right direction, I realized that more work is needed to design programs and policies that reflect the dynamic process of adolescent brain development. That work needs to extend to some of society's biggest systems—like education, health care, and the labor market—so that the landscape in which teens make their journey prioritizes their success.

So, I began reflecting on new questions: What motivates young people and how can we design intervention and prevention strategies that align with this? What are young people figuring out about themselves and how can the programs we invest in support that journey of personal discovery? What influences in their lives are most important and how can we leverage those influences for the greatest impact?

Using adolescent brain science to support youth and families opened up so many new possibilities for us at Casey. As a foundation, we started to incorporate adolescent brain science into our work to improve how we made decisions about our investments, advocacy, and research priorities. Eventually, it led to an expansion and realignment in Casey's work that became known as Thrive by 25.

Through Thrive by 25, the Foundation seeks to strengthen five essential building blocks that young people need during adolescence to be prepared to reach adulthood: basic needs, permanent caring connections, education and credentials, financial stability, and leadership opportunities.

This book is my way of extending the message of Thrive by 25 from our Casey hallways to all the people who create policies and operate programs that impact the lives of youth. I continue to be a humble student of adolescent brain science, and I hope that you will join me on this learning journey as I share insights on the way this new perspective has transformed our work and results.

Part I of this book introduces adolescent brain science in a way that I hope feels like a conversation. Many physical changes are happening in the teen brain up to age twenty-five that affect their intellectual and emotional lives. We need to go beyond understanding only the basics of puberty and sexual maturity to appreciate the many facets and nuances of adolescent brain development. It's a highly individual process for each person that is affected by their life experiences.

Circumstances like wealth, poverty, foster care, and juvenile justice can make this transition easier or more difficult for some teens. Our founder Jim Casey recognized this in his own life, and in the lives of young people working for him in the company he founded that would change the world, UPS. Having worked at UPS, I knew of Casey's story growing up in poverty to become a corporate founder and came to believe deeply in the promise of young people through his example.

Part II of the book describes the importance of each of the five Thrive by 25 areas in adolescents' lives. First, teenagers can't thrive if they don't have the basics that every human needs: a place to live, food to eat, etc. They need permanent connections to caring adults who can guide them through life's challenges. They need to gain marketable skills through education or by earning a professional credential. Access to work opportunities puts those skills into action and sets a foundation for financial stability. And as young people mature, we must equip them to develop the ability to advocate for themselves and others in ways that give them confidence, agency, and independence.

If we want equitable, and mostly excellent, life outcomes, the social structures that young people are a part of and growing up in must be constructed (or reconstructed) so that pathways, rather than barricades, are there for all. Subsequent sections of the book will acknowledge and illustrate this reality.

Part III is a call to action. Families and communities are closest to young people and play an enormous role in shaping their lives, but there are also institutional forces that have the power and potential to change adolescents' lives for the better. Nonprofits provide critical direct services and opportunities for youth leadership. Philanthropy, a smaller sector of work within nonprofits, has access to funding that can be used to spark innovation and systems change. Businesses can provide young people with access to meaningful early work experiences. Public systems like child welfare and juvenile justice can evolve their work to include building

Introduction

and strengthening the permanent connections to caring adults that adolescents urgently need. And legislators can make decisions on behalf of young people that enable the conditions for public systems to best serve young people.

I believe we as adults have certain beliefs and mindsets about teenagers and young adults that are weighing us and our work down—and, as a result, thwarting young people's ability to succeed. One of these counterproductive and incorrect beliefs is that early childhood is our only opportunity to set kids on a path to success. That is simply not true, based on what I learned in St. Louis. The research shows that the human brain in adolescence goes through immense growth and change, on par with its growth in early childhood. That means there is a second opportunity in adolescence to set young people up for success and prevent a lifetime of struggle—if we take the time and make an effort to understand the developing adolescent brain.

If our thinking about teenagers is limited to things like keeping them safe from drugs and alcohol, this can in turn limit our perspective on what's possible for young people. Sometimes these narratives and assumptions lead us to do things that can be harmful to teenagers and stunt their growth and development.

I have met and talked to hundreds of young people and system leaders over the years. I hope that their insights combined with the research that underlies this book shine a new light on ushering adolescents into adulthood in a way that is based on the science of what they need. My goal is to expand our collective thinking about what's possible for an age group that is often viewed with skepticism. If we could see young people through the lens of brain science, it could reshape the way we live and work with them—and ignite our responsibility and opportunity to support them on the road to adulthood.

I love the promise of adolescence. I hope after reading this book

Introduction

you will also fall in love with, or reaffirm your love for, teens and their still-developing brains, ripe with potential and possibility. If we get this right and change the way we approach this critical time of life, it will be an incredible, thriving legacy of which we can all be proud.

THRIVE

PART I

The Adolescent Brain

1

The Adolescent Brain

My friend and I had the opportunity to take a hike through one of the most beautiful mountain areas in northern Portugal. Our planned course that day in August 2021 was along the Paiva Walkways, a wooden pathway that winds through five miles of natural landscape. We had the right hiking shoes, bright blue skies, and about fifty other people on the journey with us. But I was still nervous. Why? The trek required that we cross a narrow suspension bridge 600 feet above a river. Yikes!

That bridge, the Arouca 516, is one of the world's longest pedestrian suspension bridges.[1] It connects the banks of the Paiva River, a popular destination for kayaking and whitewater rafting. Its design is inspired by the rope bridges built by the 13th-century Incas that spanned the cliffs and chasms of the Andes Mountains. The Arouca 516 is a stunning metallic work of art that looks like a thin silver line floating in the sky.

However intimidating the bridge looked from afar, I knew I wasn't going to cross it alone. The tour guides at the bridge gave us a brief history, shared some facts about its construction, and told us that our whole group would cross together.

The Arouca 516 is very narrow, just under four feet wide—about half the width of a typical U.S. car. This meant we would have to walk across the bridge like ants marching in a line, each hiker watching the person in front of them. Once we stepped on, each person had to keep going. There was no room to turn back.

After the instructions, it was time to cross. I followed closely behind the people in front of me, noticing that each of us crossed in our own way. One man seemed completely unfazed. He walked casually while holding a selfie stick with his camera attached, taking live video. Most others were careful and curious. I focused on looking straight ahead while clinging desperately to the handrail cables.

Even if I wanted to pause, either to gather myself or to take in the stunning view, I couldn't do it for long. I had to keep moving. When I found the courage to look around it was wondrous. A waterfall poured out between jagged rocks atop the mountains. I could see and hear birds flying overhead. The water glistened as it spilled over the rocks on the riverbed.

The local guide checked on us and encouraged us as we crossed. It was comforting to see his calm amid our collective terror. It made me believe that we would make it since he crossed the bridge dozens of times each day.

Though it felt much longer, the journey took about ten minutes. As I arrived on the other side, I felt such pride that I had overcome my reservations, delighted that I could enjoy the beautiful view from a different perspective. My fellow travelers and I all gave each other high fives. We were bonded through an experience that forced us all to navigate our vulnerability.

In so many ways, my journey across Arouca 516 mirrors the experience that most of us have as adolescents. Similar to a physical bridge, adolescence—which I define as the years between the onset of puberty to about the mid-twenties[2]—bridges two life stages: childhood and adulthood.

Bridges take people out of one place and into another. Likewise, adolescence is a developmental period that begins when the physical changes of puberty begin, taking us out of childhood.

Bridges are also a farewell, a route out of one place to another. They can force us to confront our fears. In adolescence, we bid farewell to childhood and set off on a crossing with risks and growing pains along the way as we move to the other side.

The Adolescent Brain

Crossing a bridge is a temporary experience. But for that short while, as we walk across, we have to trust that the bridge will get us where we need to go as we break from the past. Once we get to the other side of a bridge, we are at a new beginning. The same is true for human adolescents who must navigate a ten-year transition, trusting that the journey will lead to the start of a productive adulthood.

And you don't necessarily have to walk across a bridge alone. You can have a guide to show you the way like we did on Arouca 516. We parents, caregivers, and community members are the guides for young people as they enter into and move through adolescence and navigate changes in their bodies and minds.

Finally, bridges aren't just functional, but also beautiful, architectural marvels. The Arouca 516 bridge is the result of hours of research, consultation, mapping, and engineering calculations resulting in this specific design: a series of mesh trays connected to steel cables that attach to concrete V-shaped pillars that allow for clear views of the surrounding mountains.

Successfully navigating the journey of adolescence is more than celebrating a series of birthdays from teenager to young adult. It is a beautiful biological miracle of a period filled with human possibility. As I was able to do for the brief moments I could get beyond my fear and look around me on the Arouca 516 bridge, I believe all of us must recognize and honor the marvel of this wondrous developmental period of life.

None of us have a choice about moving through adolescence. All adults know from experience that to be born and alive means you go through adolescence. Human brains go through physical and chemical changes during the adolescent years, and young people are no more in charge of that process than determining how tall they will be, or when their voice will drop.

Experts have long documented that before teenagers begin to experience immense changes in their bodies and brains, they navigate another period of intense physical, intellectual, psychological, and social changes—from birth to age three. To best appreciate the shifts taking place in the adolescent brain, I think it might be useful to understand how adolescence builds upon and mirrors the first important developmental period in a young person's life: early childhood.

The Human Brain

Brains first grow and develop in utero. A normal human brain at birth weighs less than a pound.[3] As the child grows, the brain will experience two significant periods of development: the first during the initial three years of life and the second during the ten years of adolescence.

A baby's brain starts with millions of nerve cells, or neurons, that are largely not connected. Connections between neurons—which happen through tiny gaps called synapses—allow the brain to send signals and perform its functions.[4] In these early months and years, babies are developing their five senses, getting used to the world, and learning how to eat, sleep, and perform natural bodily functions. Every baby's experience of life—feeling cold or wet; crying; being held, rocked, or sung to; etc.—creates these neural connections. Whether those experiences are positive or negative, they are recorded in the brain.

I remember watching Lauren go from a baby I could hold in my arms to someone who was walking and talking and expressing a range of emotions: happiness, sadness, delight, frustration, or anger. I could see her becoming more aware of how she felt, and of the world around her.

As she practiced these skills, she moved into the phase we commonly refer to as the Terrible Twos. This is when children learn that they can say "NO!"—and they practice it loudly and repeatedly. It could be so frustrating to search for answers about her behavior. I learned that at this stage, toddlers are experiencing rapid growth in their brains and want to be more independent but still lack the vocabulary and physical skills to do so. So, that's why Lauren wasn't listening to my instructions! She wanted to try more things out for herself, a sign of her growing independence.

As frustrating as this toddler behavior is for parents to experience, there is a wealth of advice out there for parents on how to navigate it. I remember conversations among mom friends about expert advice that said this behavior is the result of a natural developmental stage that will pass. We learned that children in this age group haven't mastered the ability to use logic and words to express their feelings. They live completely in the moment.[5]

I remember how I was encouraged by my pediatrician and other moms who had been through this phase to be patient and respect this behavior as an essential and natural part of normal toddler development. I've never read a parenting blog recommending that parents chastise their toddlers if they try to say a sentence, mess up the words, get frustrated, and start to cry. Rather, parents are encouraged to console the child and help them if they want to try again.

Sometimes the oddities of this developmental period are perceived as adorable. When a toddler is learning to walk and falls, we celebrate their attempt rather than berate them for failing. As a parent, I know through experience, that if we ever feel tempted to ask a toddler about their behavior—"Why did you do that?"—we likely won't get a response. Or if we do, it won't satisfy us. We accept, sometimes begrudgingly, that tantrums and defiant behavior are in line with their age and should be expected. Toddlers can't change or skip over this stage.

While a lot of this transition is external—throwing tantrums, falling, learning to talk—a lot is happening inside toddler brains that are fueling the behaviors. Their actions and attitudes in the toddler stage are a bridge from infancy into being an older kid.[6]

As children get older, however, we are more likely to stop

celebrating them and providing positive reinforcement in the face of difficult behavior. In adolescence, our feedback can become more critical. Moreover, we tend to focus more on the physical and most visible manifestation that crossing into adolescence has begun, puberty. But at the same time, their developing brains are the invisible parts of adolescence and are changing in equally important ways. Both puberty and brain development are important to understand if we are to be the best guides to young people crossing this all-important divide.

One of the biggest mistakes we can make is to think that puberty is all there is to adolescence or assume physical maturity signals mental and emotional maturity. Since this stage is the beginning of sexual maturity and the ability to reproduce, adults tend to focus on adolescent health, concerned with preventing teen pregnancy and sexually transmitted diseases. As we observe the physical changes that are an obvious departure from childhood, we look at adolescents and believe those changes mean they are adults.

However, puberty is just one part of the psychological and physiological changes happening during the decade-long journey of adolescence. Young people can't control the pace or progress of their physical and emotional maturation, much like a toddler can't decide when he or she will hit key milestones like walking or talking. There is so much more to how young people cross the bridge into adulthood—and much of this correlates to their developing brains.

Let's take a moment to orient ourselves to the structure of the brain so that terms like "front of the brain" or "back of the brain" make sense.

The brain is made up of several sections. The stem is where the brain is attached to the spinal cord—it is where core functions for survival, like breathing and heartbeat as well as others such as producing tears or blinking, are taking place.[7]

THE ADOLESCENT BRAIN

Judgment, Reasoning, Behavior Control

CEREBRUM

The cerebrum controls multiple functions, including thinking and reasoning, speaking, judgment, problem-solving, and emotions.

The brain grows from back to front as humans pass through childhood. So, the last section of the brain that develops is responsible for what we call executive function: judgment, behavior control, and reasoning.

GROWTH STARTS HERE

CEREBELLUM

The cerebellum is at the back of the brain and controls voluntary movements, balance, posture, and fine motor skills.

BRAIN STEM

The brain stem is where the brain is attached to the spinal cord. It houses core functions for survival such as breathing and heartbeat, as well as others like producing tears or blinking.

About halfway up the back of your head is the cerebellum, which controls voluntary movements, balance, posture, and fine motor skills.

The next part of the brain is the cerebrum. It controls multiple functions including thinking and reasoning, speaking, judgment, problem-solving, and emotions.

The brain grows from back to front as humans pass through childhood. So, the last section of the brain that develops is responsible for what we call executive function: judgment, behavior control, and reasoning. Executive function refers to a set of skills. These skills underlie the capacity to plan and meet goals; regulate emotions, thoughts, and actions; follow multiple-step directions even when interrupted; and stay focused despite distractions, among others.[8]

I know the "aha" you are having. This list captures all the things that we expect (or want) teenagers and young adults to be able to do—now! No more forgotten uniforms or burnt dinner because they misheard directions, or endless giggles (or whining) during any kind of new activity.

But since the brain grows back to front, and executive function is in the front of the brain, it takes at least ten years for young people to develop these skills. In the meantime, adults lend young people some of their executive functioning—by reminding, coaching, talking through goals and dreams, and pulling them out of bed when they're late.

It takes time for our complex human brains to grow, develop, and mature into adult minds. During adolescence, the brain cells refine themselves in a natural process called pruning, which clears out connections that are no longer needed and strengthens wiring between brain cells that are important. Pruning helps the brain to build longer chains of nerve cells needed during adulthood for complex decision-making.[9]

These neurological shifts influence how young people think,

how they feel, how they behave, how they interact with everyone around them, and what motivates them. New connections within the brain create the foundation for intellectual and emotional learning and experiences that lead to maturity. These changes make young people seek independence, heighten their sensitivity to rewards, and fuel their desire to follow the influence of peers over their parents.[10]

With that in mind, consider an infant or toddler growing up and becoming a teenager. Physically they are bigger, taller, and stronger, have facial hair; or can even have a child themselves. Children of color are more likely to be mistaken for an adult years before they actually are, a process called adultification that can have devastating effects. But don't be mistaken—while a young person may look nearly grown, their physical appearance does not correlate with their level of cognitive maturity.

Given how long adolescence is, there is a range of developmental experiences taking place, based on a young person's specific age. There is a difference between young people ages fourteen to eighteen, who are navigating the end of their formal schooling and transitioning to college or work, and young people ages eighteen to twenty-four. We tend to refer to young people in those later years as young adults to reflect their growing autonomy and maturity in decision-making.

No matter where adolescents are in their transition to adulthood, I believe young people in this stage of life are entitled to the same compassion and understanding we extend to toddlers. Where are the blogs that talk about being patient and empathetic when teenagers don't want to wake up early? Or how about when they forget, again, to turn in the permission slip? Experience mood swings for seemingly no reason? Want to spend all their time with friends instead of family?

The energy and missteps caused by this natural development process generate strong emotions and opinions about adolescents.

Adult perspectives on teens and young adults are portrayed in media and pop culture and range from positive to incredibly pessimistic.

"They are curious."

"They are naive."

"They are moody."

"They are so forgetful."

"They are dangerous."

"They are disrespectful."

"They only care about social media."

And so on.

Every teenager was once an infant and a toddler we worried about keeping physically safe due to the limitations of their motor and reasoning skills.

But when the same child enters adolescence, we feel justified in our intolerance of normal developmental behaviors. Adolescence lasts twice as long as early childhood, but the internal transformation happening is no less dramatic and no less deserving of adult support and understanding.

The length of human adolescence is a unique phenomenon in nature. Harp seals—those fuzzy white creatures that look like bears and sit atop the ice in the Arctic—have a childhood that lasts about twelve days. This time consists mostly of the baby nursing from its mother as it grows from twenty-five pounds to eighty pounds. Before the end of two weeks, it is big enough to slide into the icy sea and begin life on its own.[11] Chimpanzees experience an adolescence similar to humans that includes growing big, awkward teeth, but their adolescence lasts only seven years.[12]

In other words, the ten-plus years of human adolescence—*a decade-long adventure*—gives our brains the time they need to fully grow and execute the complex decision-making of adults. Adolescence is literally what makes us human.[13]

• • •

Now that you know more about the changes happening in adolescence, let's go back to the idea of crossing the bridge from childhood to adulthood. With a ten-year journey to adulthood, it can feel like adolescents are walking across a narrow bridge that takes forever. It is just a small portion of an otherwise hopefully long life, but it can be shaky and scary as you look at the cliffs and the valley below. The crossing is unique to each person given their personality, circumstances, and biology. We all cross this bridge in different ways and at different paces.

With no standard road map to order their path, young people crossing this bridge are taking in all the tremendous possibilities ahead while managing the fear of a misstep that might send them into the valley below. When we're on this path, it doesn't feel certain that we'll make it. But once adolescence starts, young people have to keep going. There's no turning back.

One element making this journey especially precarious for young people is that they aren't given much information about what is going to happen to them. In some ways, it is like they have to cross the bridge blindfolded. We often provide young people with information about puberty, mostly out of fear of the choices they might make about their developing sexuality. But we rarely provide any information about their brain development. This makes adolescents less equipped to understand what is happening to them.

My daughter Lauren (who is in her early twenties and is still an adolescent) happened to get insight into her brain and its development during a ninth-grade biology class. A forward-thinking teacher taught a unit on brain science and explained the various developmental periods Lauren would experience. I still remember my daughter coming home excited that she knew what was happening in her body and behavior so that she could make sense of this transition. She didn't feel blind to what was going on and could give herself some grace when she didn't quite have herself together. Of course, this also gave her the knowledge to rebut any reprimand from me with, "But my prefrontal cortex isn't developed yet!" I guess knowledge is power.

I can still remember when I was pregnant and how I could sign up for weekly emails that told me everything I would want to know about my baby's development. It told me how big she was getting, what was developing, and how I could best support her growth in my womb with nutritious food, rest, and folic acid. She wasn't even born yet, but it normalized what I felt at the moment and gave me precious information to help me know what was happening.

No emails arrived when my daughter turned fourteen. Parents of adolescents rarely get much information about what to expect.

Luckily, my work experiences introduced me to adolescent brain science, which in turn illuminated my parenting experience. As a result, I was able to connect what I was learning about the developmental changes in an adolescent brain to how I could respond and engage with my daughter. It changed how I was raising her. I believe she would confirm that it helped me shift into coaching mode, creating a safe space for her to express and explore her emotions, fears, joys, and questions.

I believe we can help young people discover their unique strengths and resilience in crossing the bridge to adulthood. Adolescents encounter all kinds of circumstances as they travel this bridge. Many face barriers, like growing up in disinvested communities, discriminatory policies and practices based on the color of their skin, or limited family income. Too often these conditions determine whether children receive the resources they need to be healthy and develop on track socially, emotionally, and academically.

Part of ensuring young people can cross the bridge means removing wherever we can any obstacles that thwart safe passage. In the next chapter, I will explore some of these barriers and the devastating impact they can have on young people's development.

2

Challenges Adolescents Face

One day Lauren and I discovered a Netflix show called *Floor Is Lava*. It features a complex obstacle course with bright orange bubbling liquid that serves as the "floor." If a team of competitors safely navigates these hazards without stepping on the oozing floor, they win $10,000. Of course, the obstacles are extraordinarily difficult: a single chair that spins when contestants land on it, a slime-covered pole that they have to somehow leverage on the path toward the room's exit, and so on. Contestants can choose which way to navigate toward the exit, and every major obstacle requires collaboration: working together to swing on ropes, jump across cars, and so on.

I was drawn in, holding my breath as I watched each contestant's difficult journey to the end of the course. After a quick team meeting to devise a strategy, one team member would take the leap to navigate the first obstacle. And so on. I watched some contestants make it out by some miracle. Others got stuck or waffled on which route to take. Many of them fell into the lava and disappeared.

What a gamble. There was no single clear path to the exit and each one was littered with obstacles. The bubbling liquid floor threatens to swallow you at the first mistake, ending your opportunity to win. Witnessing the success of another team member doesn't help you because each person's strengths, circumstances, and fear factors are unique.

That got me thinking. There are approximately 100 million young people under the age of twenty-four in the United States.

The reality is that millions of them will cross the bridge to adulthood in adverse conditions akin to an obstacle course. For them, it can feel like the floor is lava.

Their futures are literally in peril if they don't make it. How can this be? What factors cause this to happen? What is that experience like for a young person? And how can we shore up the floor for every adolescent to ensure they can make the trip successfully?

The circumstances that all adolescents experience while on the road to adulthood vary greatly. There are life's ups and downs that every young person must learn to navigate through. Things like friendships changing, peer pressure, and the responsibility of learning how to make decisions on behalf of themselves. Other more challenging circumstances can happen in their lives too, such as an illness, the death of a loved one, or their parents' divorce.

Yet for many adolescents, there is a level of adversity beyond the typical rhythms of growing up, something far more serious and potentially detrimental. This kind of hardship in a young person's life is the difference between:

- having more than enough money *or* not having enough financial resources
- receiving support from caring, involved adults *or* growing up with little to no family
- being recognized for your future promise and potential *versus* being labeled a juvenile delinquent or a former foster care child
- feeling safe in your neighborhood *compared to* seeing violence in your community every day

We know through adolescent science that these kinds of harsh conditions have a physical effect on developing brains. They overstimulate the brain's stress response systems, dysregulate hormones, and over time may alter the way the brain matures—ultimately leading to poorer physical and mental health outcomes.

Persistent, continued adversity is not an optimal state for a young person (or any person) to be in for an extended time. The result for young people in this sensitive developmental period is that their brains are being shaped and molded to expect and accommodate adversity at a time when we want them to expand their horizons and prepare them to thrive into adulthood.

Researchers have seen this difference. A February 2023 study looked at the impact of childhood adversity on the brain structure of children and adolescents in Seattle.[1] About 160 youths ages eight to seventeen who had experienced adversity (defined in the study as poverty and exposure to violence) underwent MRIs for two years to measure changes in their brains. The researchers found that for the young people who had felt threatened, their prefrontal cortex was thinner in multiple areas.[2] As we learned in Chapter 1, the prefrontal cortex is responsible for several critical functions like memory, reasoning, and problem-solving. A thinner cortex could also mean an increased risk of mental health conditions. Clearly their healthy development is being placed at risk.

These impacts are avoidable and are not guaranteed to happen. Nor does this mean that the brains of young people who experience these challenges are broken or that they are damaged. Rather, the adolescent brain is elastic and growing, which means young people also are influenced by positive relationships and experiences that improve their outcomes. There is a huge opportunity to shape and temper the impact of less-than-optimal circumstances through positive experiences and multiple tries. In addition, the ability of the brain to repair itself, known as neuroplasticity, makes it possible for young people to overcome adversity on their journey to adulthood.[3] But the optimal path is to avoid this risk and repair altogether.

If we are to support all young people on their journey to adulthood, we must understand the depth of hardship that some adolescents face along the way. With more insight into their experiences, we can work to prevent these circumstances and better help adolescents manage and recover from these potentially derailing events when they do happen. The healthy development of their brains and the future positive outcome of their lives are at stake.

Adversity is a general term. Researchers who have studied the challenges young people face generally group them into these three general categories: adverse childhood experiences, toxic stress, and trauma.

Adverse Childhood Experiences (ACE)
All experiences, including negative ones, shape young brains that are growing and developing. A groundbreaking study showed just how much negative childhood experiences have shaped lives in future decades. The term ACE, or adverse childhood experience, came to be after a published study from the Centers for Disease Control and Prevention (CDC) and Kaiser Permanente, the California-based health care organization.[4]

Years earlier, doctors working at the health care company stumbled on a relationship between the rate of adults who dropped out of an obesity program and their emotional experiences as children. In interviews, the adults who didn't lose weight talked about why, and many of their reasons pointed to difficult childhood experiences. For example, one woman described a sexual assault she experienced as a young adult that caused her to gain more than one hundred pounds the following year.[5]

Dr. Vincent Felitti and his colleagues wanted to know more. They interviewed more than 17,000 adults on the health plan and asked questions in eight categories about difficult or adverse experiences in childhood. These questions included the following:

Did you experience repeated physical, emotional, or sexual abuse?

Did you grow up in a house with someone who abused alcohol or drugs or was in prison?

Did you live with someone who was chronically depressed, mentally ill, or suicidal?

At home, was your mother treated violently?

Were your parents separated, divorced, or in some way lost to you growing up?

The results found a significant relationship between an adult's physical and emotional health and what happened to them as children. Adults who had a high number of adverse childhood experiences also had poor physical and mental outcomes like diabetes, depression, heart disease, and substance abuse in adulthood.[6] That correlation between ACEs and future outcomes revealed something new and powerful: Safe and nurturing childhood environments are a foundation for an individual's future health outcomes and can make for a healthier society.

That means there are high stakes for making sure young people have positive childhood experiences and for preventing negative ones. Yet ACEs are extremely common. According to the CDC, between 2011 and 2020, about 64 percent of U.S. adults reported they had experienced at least one type of ACE before age eighteen, and nearly 1 in 6 (17.3 percent) reported they had experienced four or more types of ACEs.[7]

On their journey to adulthood, ACEs are for some young people like carrying heavy weights in their backpacks as they make the trip. Any child can experience an ACE, and a majority of children experience at least one. However, some young people are more likely to have an ACE because of their racial identity and their family's social, economic, and historical environment. Across the country, 61 percent of Black non-Hispanic children and 51 percent of Hispanic children have experienced at least one ACE, compared with 40 percent of white non-Hispanic children and only 23 percent of Asian non-Hispanic children.[8]

When it comes to two or more ACEs, youth of color have experienced them at higher rates: Native American (37 percent), African American (24 percent), Hispanic or Latino (19 percent), white (15 percent), and Asian (6 percent). ACEs may be common, but the impacts are not evenly distributed across racial and ethnic groups.

Although ACEs are common among children, and more common in certain groups, it is not always guaranteed that an ACE will have a long-term negative effect. Some things can promote healing and resilience, known as protective factors: having the presence of an adult who makes a child feel safe, adequate social support in the form of a loving, stable adult, and living in a safe and supportive neighborhood.[9] That's why these ingredients are core to the Annie E. Casey Foundation's strategy and are embedded in Thrive by 25.

Dr. Bruce D. Perry, a noted American psychiatrist and expert on ACEs, describes the impact of mitigating factors when he tells the story of a patient named Ally who had to navigate the loss of her parents under very tragic circumstances. When Ally was four, her father murdered her mother.

Ally lived in what Perry describes as a close-knit community. After losing both her parents in this tragic way, she moved in with one of her aunts and was surrounded by family, including cousins, aunts, uncles, and grandparents. Ally was also active in her church, played sports, and had supportive teachers in school. All of the adults in her life knew what happened to her and how to support her.

Ally went to therapy to help her heal, but Perry reported that over time, Ally had to attend therapy less—from three times a week to once a week. She also continued to do well in school and extracurricular activities. She was still without both her parents, but she was able to continue to grow emotionally and physically within the bonds of her extended family and community.

Evidence shows a relationship between the long-term impact of an adverse childhood experience and the presence of a trusted adult for a young person throughout the experience. A group of UK psychiatrists surveyed adults who had experienced four or more ACEs and found that they were more likely to have a poor diet, smoke daily, and drink alcohol more heavily if they did not have the support of a trusted adult in childhood.[10]

Both individual experiences and data show what is possible when a young person who endures an adverse childhood experience has support to facilitate their recovery. They confirm that support is most effective when it's delivered in the context of relationships, extended family, and community. Adults must provide sustained support and opportunities for self-development close to the time the adverse experience occurs so that healing can begin. When those things happen, the young person can learn to manage their emotions and move through the experience with a sense of resilience.

But when adults don't provide sustained support and opportunities, the repercussions from an adverse childhood experience can fester. Adolescents with higher ACE scores are impacted mentally and physically, which can have a cumulative effect, especially if their family environment does not moderate the impact.[11] This situation could leave the young person under constant pressure without an escape. That unrelenting pressure is known as toxic stress, and it has consequences for the developing brains of children.

Toxic Stress

Children need to learn how to cope with adversity; it is a normal part of life and growing up. Some challenges are helpful for children to learn healthy coping skills. But more intense or prolonged stress brings lasting harmful effects that can inhibit growth and development.

Because children need reassurance from caring adults in managing their emotions, a child's response when stress is present depends on how well adults respond to them. In other words, children rely on interaction with adults to help them learn and develop a healthy stress management response.

Normal stress, also known as positive stress, would be something like getting an injection at a doctor's appointment. After a brief moment of elevated heart rate and an increase in stress hormones, the body returns to normal.

One level up from normal stress is tolerable stress. The response to tolerable stress is more intense than normal stress, for example, dealing with the loss of a loved one or managing a physical injury. While it may be more intense, with the response and reassurance of caring adults, the child can manage or tolerate the stress and get back to a level where they can recover and not suffer lasting effects on their bodies or their brains.

Toxic stress happens when a young person feels pressure from the adversity that they are facing, and that pressure doesn't let up or isn't supported by an adult who can help a young person return to a normal state. If the stress builds up, and there are no relationships that the child can draw on as a buffer, then physical and emotional impacts can reverberate.[12]

I've heard young people describe to me difficult situations in which they experienced toxic stress such as the following:

- A young person cycling through multiple foster homes, having the repeated experience of packing up their belongings into plastic bags with little notice and unaware of their destination or who will be there.

- In a family experiencing homelessness, children struggling to do homework hunched night after night over a bed in a cramped local shelter.
- A child living through a natural disaster then starting over at a new school in a new city while still grieving the loss of their home, their friendships, their toys, and everything familiar.

Thousands of young people are living in these kinds of situations and others like them. Their pathway to recovery could be compromised if they also have no stable or consistent adult relationships upon which to rely.

There are many reasons young people find themselves without these relationships. The adults may not be physically present. Or they might be too overwhelmed by systemic challenges like racism, poverty, or community violence to model for their children the emotional regulations that they need. Or the young person may find themselves ostracized by the adults in their lives because of their sexual identity.

When comforting activities are also absent—like playing outside, riding bicycles, talking about their day with family around a dinner table, or being able to participate in school activities without fear of discrimination—young people endure toxic stress with no relief.

A child who has no means of acknowledging or addressing the adverse experience at home, in school, or with the help of any trusted adult remains alone in their difficult emotional experiences. And if in that state they experience trauma, that adds to their challenges.

Trauma
These days, we seem to hear people use the word trauma to describe any sort of difficult situation. The official use of this term, however, is to describe a certain type of experience.

When it comes to children and young adults, trauma is defined as an event that feels frightening, dangerous, or violent and poses a threat to life or body. Also, because children are so dependent on their caregivers as a source of safety, they can find it traumatic to witness the security or life of someone they love threatened.[13]

An example of trauma is a young person who consistently witnesses shootings of community members in their neighborhood. In a moment, they could lose a friend or elder they know. As neighborhood violence continues, they will likely develop strong fears of bodily harm for themselves and become desensitized to grief and loss.

Trauma can certainly refer to a specific event like losing a parent, even when multiple people who experience the same event have different reactions to it. If two siblings suffer the loss of a parent, one might find it extremely traumatic and struggle to recover while the other sibling bounces back more quickly. Trauma can also refer to the emotional response to a prolonged adverse experience, like ongoing violence.[14]

While family is supposed to be a source of refuge and strength for young people, the circumstances within and among family members can cause a traumatic experience. A young person may have been born to parents who were unable to take care of them due to addiction or incarceration—leaving them struggling with feelings of abandonment. Or they could have grown up in an unstable home due to emotional or physical abuse, or in any environment where their interests and talents were not carefully nurtured and supported. Instances where a young person was emotionally or physically neglected by a caregiver are also a source of trauma.

Research shows that the young people who are more likely to have adverse experiences—Native, African American, and Latino youth—are also more likely to have experienced trauma. There are groups of young people with specific experiences—like youth growing up in foster care and the juvenile justice system—who have had traumatic experiences even before they entered into those systems. They are also at risk of having traumatic experiences once they are there, depending on the living situations they are placed in. A child who is separated from a parent or caregiver and goes to a stranger's home, no matter the circumstances requiring that urgent change, finds the separation traumatic.

Trauma changes the journey to adulthood because it changes the brain. How the adolescent brain develops when it has experienced trauma is different from a brain that has not.

Since trauma represents an overwhelming state, children (like adults) seek ways to cope. Young people do this in their own ways, like crying and denying that the stress is happening. Young people can also seek outside sources to distract themselves from trauma, like constantly watching electronic devices. Some soothing strategies are helpful and may even be productive in comforting the young person. However, other strategies may become harmful or counterproductive if a child uses distraction strategies repeatedly as an escape or moves to abusing substances or self-harm. Often young people find that these kinds of coping mechanisms do not work, or their effectiveness wears off.

Who Is Impacted?

No adolescent is immune from undergoing emotional hardships, and they require love and support from adults to manage the experience. It is also clear that certain groups of young people are more likely to experience ACEs, toxic stress, and trauma. It is worth exploring what it is that creates so much harm in these young people's lives.

Millions of adolescents do not have the foundation of a healthy childhood, which affects their behavior and development. Healthy adolescence requires certain experiences, opportunities, and support. When those are missing and instead are replaced with stressors, lack of guidance, and limited opportunities, the result is a delayed or derailed adolescence.

In other words, adversities put healthy development at risk. We at the Casey Foundation are most concerned about young people who are trying to make it through adolescence with multiple challenges that jeopardize their future. It is important to understand what that feels and looks like in order to deepen our understanding so we can help adolescents.

The young people to be most concerned about are those who are low income, especially youth of color, youth growing up in high-poverty communities, youth with experience in the juvenile justice system, youth who are also parents, and youth who have experience in the child welfare system.

If a family's annual income falls below 50 percent of the poverty guidelines, they are classified as being in "deep poverty." There are 17.9 million people, or 5.5 percent of the U.S. population, who are in deep poverty, according to the Population Reference Bureau.[15]

Poverty complicates every aspect of a child's experience, from hunger impacting their ability to learn to the familial stresses of struggling to meet basic needs. It can impact a young person's opportunity to take part in extracurricular activities when the family's priority is survival. Young people who are living in families struggling with poverty are enduring the toxic stress that comes from not having a safe, basic place to live and enough food to eat. I will talk more about the implications of unmet basic needs in Chapter 4.

Youth who are involved in the juvenile justice system experience adversity that is extremely complex as they are isolated from their families in a punitive setting, usually with little discussion of rehabilitation or understanding of how the developing adolescent brain views risk and reward. Accountability for juvenile crime is necessary, but it must be balanced with a focus on creating positive developmental opportunities so these young people can create a different future for themselves. There is also an opportunity to prevent young people from coming into the system through positive opportunities that develop their sense of self and purpose. I will talk more about this in Part II of the book.

For youth who are already in the juvenile justice system, their rehabilitation can be threatened by additional trauma young people often experience once they enter. Youth placed in these kinds of institutionalized settings are at a high risk of being abused. In 2010, the Bureau of Justice Statistics confirmed an epidemic of sexual abuse by surveying more than 26,000 youth in facilities. At least 3,000, or 12 percent, reported being victimized by staff or other youth.[16]

For young adults who are involved in the criminal justice system, a majority have had more than one ACE, according to the Justice Policy Institute. For example, as a seventeen-year-old girl, Roszetta Timons defended herself against a rapist—her brother who had abused her for years—and killed him. She went to prison for twenty-six years. Timons said as she served her sentence, beginning from when she was a juvenile, she never was asked about her traumas or received any support.[17] This is a huge, missed opportunity to support young people while they go through the criminal justice system.

Birth rates for adolescents ages fifteen to nineteen have fallen more than 50 percent, but there are still teen parents.[18] For these young people who are adjusting to being new parents as their brains are still developing, the need for support in their caretaker role is high. As young parents, they are still maturing in their ability to be responsible, find stable employment, and secure a safe place to live. Young parents need extra support and opportunities to address any ACEs that may have led to early parenthood.

Finally, in fiscal year 2022, there were 91,644 young people ages of fourteen and twenty-one living in foster care—about a quarter of all children in foster care that year.[19] These youth face significant challenges. They have experienced the grief and trauma of being separated from their families, compounded by the trauma they often endure in a safety-first child welfare system that is not designed to support their adolescent need for growing independence. Additionally, many older foster youths are not growing up in loving private homes but in group care settings. These institutions rarely foster interpersonal relationships that create a sense of safety and nurturing. Together, these circumstances make a youth in foster care more likely to be the victim of abuse, with up to 40 percent of former foster youth reporting that they were abused.[20]

There are ways for young people to manage these kinds of adversity. In subsequent chapters, we will talk about some of the ways that can happen with support from adults. Part of the formula is building and improving the systems that serve children to focus on supporting family strengths and preventing adverse childhood experiences, trauma, and toxic stress. With each precious young life at stake, we can't accept failure.

Especially in difficult circumstances, young people need opportunities to see and create a path forward. A field of practice called positive youth development involves creating spaces, opportunities, training, and relationships that take advantage of a young person's strengths. This allows them to have greater clarity about what kind of life they want to create as adults.

When confronted with the data about how many young people are struggling on the road to adulthood, we often hear the narrative of a single individual who overcame difficult odds to "make it." Sometimes it's a child who has survived a seemingly insurmountable family tragedy and gets accepted into all Ivy League colleges with a full scholarship; other times, it's a millionaire who overcame poverty in childhood. We often feel inspired by these individual examples of extraordinary personal transformation. They seem to validate an unspoken social rule that individual victory over impossible circumstances is possible through sheer individual effort. From this notion of "bootstraps" and hard work springs the idea that no one has an excuse to be defeated by their circumstances.

My life could look like one of those individual success stories. I was born and grew up in the South at a time when the doors to opportunities for Black people were just opening and there was still a lot of discrimination in housing, education, and community investment. Yet, I excelled. I participated in prestigious enrichment programs, graduated from high school, and went on to earn college and law degrees. I worked in corporate America for years before becoming the first African American person to lead the Casey Foundation.

But I wasn't homeless, a teen parent, or navigating the child welfare or juvenile justice systems. I lived with two professional parents in a stable middle-class Black neighborhood free from crime and violence. There were normal bumps on my journey to adulthood, but I had a lot of invisible tailwinds working in my favor.

The adolescent developing brain needs positive experiences to grow and thrive. And while a single example of someone succeeding without them might be inspiring, it misses the point for several reasons.

An individual-focused approach is not part of the recipe for a thriving society. Instead of leveraging the strengths, resources, and connections that spring forth from the community, it places a heavy burden on the backs of young people to endure and figure things out on their own. That leads to isolation and damaging emotional pressure we shouldn't want millions of young people to endure.

But right now, that's exactly what is happening. We generally have a societal system where the random success of individual lives serves as a compass to guide young people through obstacles as they journey toward adulthood. We might even do it inside of families by comparing cousins or one sibling to another. If you are reading this, you are willing to disrupt this approach.

At the Annie E. Casey Foundation, we don't accept the devastating effects of adversity on young people as a given. Many programs and organizations focus on helping them emerge victorious when circumstances are stacked against them. But there is another way: By changing the systems and policies that govern families' lives, that's how we change the odds.

In the next chapter, I will begin to describe what system change is as it relates to young people. It is at the heart of what we do at the Casey Foundation, and it is tied to our earliest beginnings and our founder, Jim Casey. For a deeper understanding, it is helpful to know how Jim Casey saw the world and his work—which became the motivations for his philanthropy.

3

A New Approach

The first time I heard the name Jim Casey—the founder of the shipping company UPS and the foundation that I lead—was when I joined UPS in 1996. All new employees attend an orientation program for a week or so that explores the origins of the company and the values that continue to drive it.

I learned that Jim had a tough life growing up in Seattle, Washington. He had dropped out of school at age eleven to help earn money for his family when his father died.[1] He found work as a messenger delivery boy—a job that he could do with his limited education—and it taught him the value of an on-time delivery. This realization complemented what his parents had already taught him about the all-important values of courtesy, dependability, and integrity.

When Jim was nineteen years old, he teamed up with another messenger, Claude Ryan, and they started the "American Messenger Company" on August 28, 1907. This was a grand name for just a few messengers, but it reflected their big ambitions. They borrowed $100 to get started from Jim Brewster, a friend of Claude's uncle, Charlie. Eventually, through some changes and evolution, United Parcel Service was born on Valentine's Day 1919.[2]

With UPS, Jim Casey created a first-of-its-kind system for quickly shipping packages around the world. This new approach required speed despite a high volume of individually wrapped and differently sized items going to different places. It also required that packages travel on all kinds of modes of transportation: trains, planes, and tractor-trailers between cities, to trucks and motorcycles within cities, to even gondolas in Italy. Each part of the system must communicate and work in concert to get any individual package where it is going.

I saw the UPS system up close in my fourteen years at the company. I served in a variety of roles but the most memorable was when I worked as a UPS driver. I experienced firsthand the care and efficiency UPS uses to manage packages and meet customer expectations. And I learned from that experience that a high-functioning complex system is possible and there is a lot we can learn from corporate best practices to better serve youth and young adults.

I had just started a new role as a lobbyist for the company. My boss believed that experience as a UPS driver would enhance my ability to represent the company with legislators and regulators. At first, I balked at the idea. But I soon left the cushy confines of our lobbying office to put on a uniform and drive the big brown truck.

For three months I delivered packages in Waldorf, Maryland, south of Washington, D.C., during the 2005 Christmas season. It turned out to be one of the most transformative professional experiences I have ever had. My route was about one mile long in a light mixed-use industrial commercial area next to a shopping mall. I picked up and delivered from a range of businesses: doctor's offices, law firms, an upholstery shop, a car repair garage, a trophy store, McDonald's, and a major picture frame retailer. About 10 percent of my stops were residential. I made about 150 stops a day.

I remember reading the labels on the packages I carried, deeply fascinated that the items I was delivering that day might have been sent the previous day from places near and far, from Baltimore to Beijing. To make this possible, the shipping and sorting processes in our package sorting centers were precisely designed and near-flawlessly executed to the minute. My role was to be responsible for the final leg of the package journey, the delivery.

Before I delivered every package, I scanned it with a small

A New Approach

handheld computer to create up-to-the-moment accurate tracking information that was sent to UPS and the shippers awaiting package status updates. But I must confess that I wasn't the most efficient driver. On days when it was clear that I would not complete my deliveries, I had to call my supervisor so that other drivers could arrive and help deliver what I could not.

I learned what is possible in a well-orchestrated process and how much technology and automation facilitate it. I also learned that it was impossible to do important work alone and that help was often required. Those three months profoundly shaped my view on what is possible both in corporate America and in our country.

After fourteen years, I left UPS and accepted a job as vice president of external affairs at the Annie E. Casey Foundation. I was drawn to the opportunity to use all that I'd learned as a corporate executive and apply it in service of a different kind of mission—improving the lives of children and families.

When Jim Casey and his siblings, George, Henry, and Marguerite, created the Foundation, they wanted to name it after their mother as a reflection of their belief that children succeed when their parents can provide emotional and material support. It was more than an aspiration, but the truth of their lives. They wanted to create that experience of love and support in the lives of other children and young people.

"She always kept our clothes clean and mended, and had a warm, nourishing meal ready, regardless of the hour at which we were able to get home from work to eat it," Jim Casey said. "Mother gave us encouragement and inspiration and she instilled in us a code of ethics, without which I hate to think what might have happened in later years."[3]

The Foundation was a way to honor their family's humble beginnings and to put their financial success from UPS to use in a way that helped young people succeed—similar to the way Annie E. Casey nurtured her four children. The Foundation gave out smaller grants when it first began, and then one group of young people captured Casey's attention and permanently shifted the foundation's focus: children in foster care.

Casey's interest in foster care can be traced to a problem that stumped him: young employees who were in dire straits and unable to make ends meet and who stole from the company. He was no longer running UPS's day-to-day operations, and he had time to interview the young workers. He discovered a common thread: Many of them had either been raised or spent time in foster care. They told him about moving multiple times, having to live in different families, and being in the care of unprepared or uncaring caretakers.

Casey wanted to learn more and found critical insight from the Child Welfare League of America. As he came to understand that many problems stem from ineffective child welfare systems, he decided to take up the cause for reform guided by all that he had learned as an innovative business leader.

When I joined the Casey Foundation, I carried with me the experience of participating in a high-functioning system that carefully tracked and protected goods. I was excited and eager about the work, yet dismay began to creep in.

Each day as I learned more in my new role, I realized that things were much different in the systems designed to serve children and families compared to the high-functioning corporate system designed to move packages. Differences like the following:

Well-paid employees and fully staffed teams? Rare. Organizations and public agencies working with the most vulnerable populations were chronically understaffed with low employee pay.

Stable, consistent leadership so that successes can build and grow? No. Rather, constant turnover was the norm—the average tenure of a child welfare leader is eighteen months.

Real-time tracking through effective and updated data systems? Not quite. Data from child-serving systems were typically two to three years behind, which constantly forced leaders to make decisions based on outdated information.

Convenient locations for families to access services? You can print UPS shipping labels at home and drop off a package at multiple locations along the path of your errands. Meanwhile, many families have to trek by public transportation—which can be unreliable and expensive—to social services offices far from their homes during work hours.

Aligned agencies that work together seamlessly to coordinate services for families? Seldom, if ever. A single package in the UPS system often travels by plane, train, and truck—all coordinated by the company, not customers. A family that needs food, housing, and unemployment insurance encounters three different systems that don't interact.

A clear vision by organizations and public systems for how they want the lives of the families they serve to be positively impacted? I would describe it as a persistent survival approach to delivering services. Meanwhile, at UPS it was ingrained in us to create a superior experience that was customer-first, implemented by dedicated employees, and driven by innovation.

Jim Casey's approach to solving problems, both business and social issues, was rooted in examining the systems that undergird them and then finding ways to improve those systems. That initial curiosity about how the foster care system served young people is at the root of the foundation's focus and investment in foster care that continues today. He chose to look at systems because he knew that they were the most effective and efficient way to make change with far-reaching ripple effects.

At the Annie E. Casey Foundation, we also believe in a tailored approach for supporting adolescents and their families, rather than a one-size-fits-all. A growing body of scientific knowledge about the adolescent brain has created a greater understanding of what young people need to thrive into adulthood. This provides the evidence-based rationale for treating adolescence as the unique development period that it is. We have used adolescent brain science to develop new ideas about what young people need to thrive into adulthood.

We have taken those ideas based on adolescent brain science and put them into a five-part framework called Thrive by 25.[4] Looking back on Jim Casey's childhood, he had each of those five pillars that enabled him to be successful into adulthood:

Basic Needs: His mother made sure the family had food, clothing, shelter, and enough for the necessities.

Permanent Caring Connections: His close connection to his mother and bond with his siblings and close family friends provided support that kept the family together. He also had mentors who believed and invested in his business.

Education and Credentials: Jim Casey had enough of a strong foundation in math and reading and came of age in an era where he could drop out of school to work and still be successful, learning life lessons that shaped his career choice to become an entrepreneur.

Financial Stability and Well-being: Jim Casey earned money for his family and also started a business at the age of nineteen that would become UPS. He also benefited from someone who could provide a small business loan, having access to safe non-predatory financial tools.

Youth Leadership: Jim Casey learned to be a leader as his small bicycle messenger business grew.

I view the Thrive by 25 framework that is focused on improving the lives of teenagers and young adults as a fitting tribute to the man who started UPS as an adolescent.

The data show that as a society, we are not delivering the services and support that young people need to be successful. The "we" is the public infrastructure of health care, schools, out-of-school programming, social services, nutrition, childcare, and housing that is supposed to exist to serve children and adults in need. The clarity

A New Approach

of adolescent brain science is a powerful guide for the leaders of all kinds of systems to improve the design and delivery of the services and opportunities young people need.

Nearly 16.4 million children are growing up in poverty in families unable to meet their basic needs.[5] We don't deliver millions of children to adulthood successfully because we allow them to be burdened by multiple layers of challenges. UPS would go out of business if it failed to deliver 16.4 million packages to their destination. I know that we can do better.

I know how a system is supposed to work because I've seen it up close through the world's largest package delivery system. That experience and knowledge have never left me. They influence to this day how I lead the Casey Foundation and our work on behalf of improving the lives of all children and young people.

It is clear to me that the core issues the Annie E. Casey Foundation has come to focus on—strengthening families, increasing economic opportunity, and developing more supportive environments for kids—are not separate endeavors. I believe strongly that we need to break down the silos that exist in the ways our country supports kids and families. We need to help leaders across multiple systems, places, and issues innovate in more effective ways. We also need to reshape the narrative around adolescence and help more people understand that it's an important developmental period much like early childhood where the brain is open to learning and growing.

We can collectively do so much to ensure that all young people have what they need as they cross the bridge to adulthood. We also have a wealth of science and research that informs how programs and policies can support that journey.

Now that we understand the adolescent brain and how important and unique this development period is, we can meet the needs of adolescents so they are equipped for their journey. In Part II, I will take a deeper look at each of the five components of a healthy adolescence.

PART II

The Components of a Healthy Adolescence

4

Basic Needs

As we developed our approach to Thrive by 25 at Casey, we identified our desired result: improving the outcomes for adolescents and young adults ages fourteen to twenty-four. But what specific outcomes should we choose? We thought we knew, based on several factors: our research experience honed over decades; volumes of data about effective prevention and intervention strategies; and wisdom gleaned from grantee and partner organizations in the fields that serve young people. We settled on the following: connections in meaningful relationships, education, college/work, and taking on leadership roles in their lives and for others.

But we were wrong.

Not completely wrong, we learned, but we certainly missed a critical issue.

We had invited young people to a focus group meeting to hear their direct feedback on improving outcomes for their lives. We wanted to test our theories and working ideas about what we thought young people needed against the reality of what they were experiencing in their lives.

One young man told us he watched his best friend get shot and die in the street while in high school. He had managed to graduate and start college but was struggling to heal from that trauma and loss. He said it made focusing on anything else nearly impossible. Would our strategy address this challenge?

Additional questions emerged: What if a young person doesn't have stable housing? What if they don't know where their next meal is coming from? These were not hypothetical scenarios, the young people said. Hunger and living in an unsafe place were unfortunately a current reality that several were facing. Many described the anxiety and depression they struggled with as a result.

Food. Housing. Mental and physical health. Safety. These were the things that were weighing on young people. It was clear, based on their feedback, that we needed to adjust our Thrive by 25 priorities to include one more focus area: basic needs. We hadn't fully appreciated the impact that not having these basic needs met was having on young people in their transition to adulthood; if we wanted any of the other areas we planned to invest in to become a reality, we had to put basic needs first. The young people in the focus groups illuminated that for us. By meeting their basic needs first, young people would be better able to focus on school, graduate, pursue college or work, and be prepared to make a difference in their communities—all steps we identified as critical for them to pass through to thrive into adulthood.

When basic needs go unmet, young people spend their valuable energy in survival mode. Addressing their basic needs requires absolute focus on the present, which jeopardizes their ability to plan for the future.

Their revelations and realities forced us to dig deeper. We needed to understand what they defined as basic needs and how low-income youth and families use government and nonprofit support to fill the gaps when they or their families lack the money to make ends meet. Figuring out how to survive month after month takes a toll and impacts so many other things in an adolescent's life. Given the scope of the challenge, we needed to consider how to solve this issue in a systemic way that serves the millions in need.

What Are Basic Needs?

The concept of basic needs has been discussed across various fields including economics, sociology, and psychology, as they are considered universal for human survival and thriving.

The young people in our focus group brought to life a concept first introduced in 1943 by American psychologist Abraham Maslow to explain human motivation, the Hierarchy of Needs. Maslow believed that all humans could become self-actualized, or in other words, their best selves.

For a person to become self-actualized, Maslow wrote, meant that they had "the full use and exploitation of talents, capacities, and potentialities."[1] This is exactly what we want for all young people.

The route to getting there involves moving through a hierarchy of needs beginning from those most vital for survival, then pursuing other higher-level needs that are more social and emotional. Without first meeting the foundational needs, it is unlikely or more difficult to later achieve the higher-level needs. While there have been some critiques and challenges to this structure—including that it

Maslow's
HIERARCHY OF NEEDS

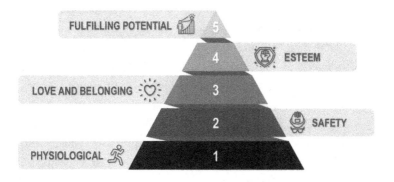

is Western-focused and individualistic[2]—the fact that Maslow argues for the importance of addressing urgent needs first is difficult to completely dismiss.

Maslow used a pyramid to delineate these needs. The most basic, physiological human needs are at the bottom: air, food, water, heat, clothes, and the basic biological functions of the body. The most basic needs, according to Maslow, also include personal safety—a sense that one's body won't experience harm.

The next higher level of the pyramid addresses psychological needs. As individuals interact with others in friendships and other relationships, they seek feelings of belonging and love. Maslow describes an individual's personal need for self-esteem and feelings of accomplishment.

The final cluster of needs, according to Maslow, is at the top of the pyramid. They relate to achieving one's purpose, utilizing your full potential, and the capacity for creative expression.

As I reflected on feedback from our focus group, our strategy was so focused on the top two tiers of Maslow's pyramid—feelings and purpose—that we had mistakenly skipped over the foundation. The young people drew our attention back to basic needs as a critical ingredient to achieving the higher aspirations they have.

Food, shelter, health care, safety, and technology: The impact of having even one of these basic needs unmet is difficult to endure and threatens adolescent development. However, the tragic reality is that in the United States, a large percentage of young people have a childhood and adolescence that is marked by a persistent lack of critical resources. Having your basic needs met is not a given.

The concept of basic needs is a vital building block for crossing the bridge into adulthood. Imagine this as the difference between crossing the bridge barefoot and wearing proper hiking boots. So many young people experience material hardship that they step into adolescence without the minimum required gear needed to make the journey. And for a voyage that takes at least ten years, we need to ensure that all young people have what they need to not only start the crossing but also complete it.

Let's dive deeper into each area of basic needs to describe its significance for teens and young adults and the impact of deprivation.

Food

A growling stomach is something we all have experienced. But what if that stomach stays empty for one meal, then two, then four? What happens when a teenager or young adult is hungry and there is no food to eat? That is the reality for nearly 7.3 million children and youth in the United States.[3]

For too many young people, hunger affects every aspect of their lives. Studies have linked child hunger to lower grades in school and lower scores on standardized tests. It has also been shown to increase anxiety and depression, which affects focus and the ability to learn.

Having insufficient food available is not limited to children under age eighteen. It is a persistent issue for many college students, too. Imagine graduating from high school, and then as you strive to navigate all the hurdles that are part of the college experience—taking multiple classes, studying for exams, tackling daily stresses with no immediate financial support—your efforts are hampered by hunger.

The Hope Center for College, Community, and Justice at Temple University releases data and advocates on behalf of college students and food. The center says meeting the basic needs of college students provides several key benefits: supporting student success in the classroom, enhancing a student's ability to graduate, and their basic humanity. A survey of 86,000 college and university students across 123 campuses found that 41 percent of students at four-year institutions and 48 percent of students at two-year institutions experienced food insecurity in the thirty days preceding the survey. More than half of the respondents at two-year colleges and 44 percent of respondents at four-year colleges worried about running out of food.[4] That is a startling number of young people facing a huge hurdle to obtaining a postsecondary degree.

Housing
Without housing, everything else is much more difficult. Housing is critical because families that live in consistent housing can provide the structure, routines, and reliability their children need to grow. Separately, youth who are disconnected from their parents because they become pregnant or are LGBTQ+ can also be without stable housing. There are an estimated 4.2 million youth and young adults who are homeless, with about 700,000 of them on their own without a parent or guardian.[5]

Housing instability—which can include being forced to move frequently, eviction, having no fixed place to stay, or the experience of homelessness—does the opposite. It increases household stress, including for children. This causes their developing brains to produce more of the stress hormone cortisol, triggered by fight-or-flight mode. Chronic and persistent release of cortisol eventually destroys brain connections needed for learning and relationship building.[6]

Lack of housing also affects safety and dignity because you are without access to running water, heat in the winter, cool air in the summer, clean clothes, and a place to bathe. When all these aspects of housing are absent, studies have shown that it affects a young person's mental health and school performance. For example, the national average graduation rate for homeless students was 68 percent in the 2020–21 school year—12 percentage points below other low-income students and nearly 18 percentage points below all students.[7]

The link between housing instability and educational success becomes more pronounced when one considers how moving, sometimes multiple times a year, could mean a new school, a new teacher, and a new social environment for a student. The National

Academy of Sciences has noted that in high-poverty urban schools, more than half of their students can turn over within a single school year.[8] This instability, the report notes, makes reforms like smaller classes, better-trained teachers, and modern facilities irrelevant. The impact of this turnover is not just on the students who move but on the stability of the whole school community given this high level of churn.

A different study from the National Longitudinal Study of Adolescent to Adult Health looked at the long-term impact on adolescents who had housing instability. That study found that adolescents who reported multiple addresses over twelve months were more likely to smoke, have depression, or be arrested. According to the researchers, "Instability has unique impacts on adolescents across a variety of domains that endure into adulthood."[9] Adolescents are extremely sensitive to family stability, which is largely based upon a safe place to live.

It is worth noting that the poverty that often drives housing instability also puts many families at a high risk of being investigated by child welfare authorities for neglect. A family that doesn't have access to running water or heat may be accused of providing an unsafe home for children. So, when families aren't supported to find affordable housing, some portion of their children will end up in foster care, separated from family members whom they love.

In 2023, the United States had a shortage of more than 7 million affordable housing units, and there is no state in the country where a renter working full-time at minimum wage can afford a two-bedroom apartment.[10] Nowhere. That makes housing instability much more than a risk. It is a reality.

Mental and Physical Health
Without glasses, how can a child with impaired vision see the board while in school?

How focused on the teacher is a teenager suffering from a toothache due to a lack of dental care?

How many days of school will a child with asthma miss without proper treatment?

Health care is a basic need that impacts everything about a young person's ability to focus, learn, and be without physical pain as they grow up and move through adolescence. The pitfalls for young people not having their health needs addressed are many. This was exacerbated by the COVID-19 pandemic, with its forced isolation and economic stressors leading to an adverse effect on both the physical and mental well-being of adolescents.[11]

Although adolescence is widely considered to be a period of optimal physical health, the rapid physical, cognitive, and social changes that teens experience can be associated with the onset of significant health problems. Poor nutrition and inadequate exercise contribute to obesity and its related effects on health. Mental health conditions are also a concern for adolescents. Approximately 1 in 8 adolescents and young adults in the United States live with depression, and suicide is one of the most common causes of death in this age group.[12]

In Part I, I explained how neurological shifts in the adolescent brain influence how young people think, feel, and behave. Their brains have a heightened sensitivity to the dopamine produced by risk-taking that makes young people seek out new experiences. Those attributes can be a recipe for adolescents being more likely to engage in high-risk behaviors. Although use of alcohol, tobacco, and most illicit drugs among American teens has declined in recent years, there is a substantial increase in the use of tobacco and marijuana vaping products. In addition, adolescents are likely to be sexually active when their peers are—and even when they *believe* their peers are (whether it is true or not).[13]

All of this points to the critical need for young people to have access to health care, either through their parents or other means.

Publicly funded insurance is an option for many low-income families, but only some financially struggling families will meet eligibility requirements. On the road to adulthood, health is a precursor to wealth.

Safety

For too many young people, feeling safe is an elusive experience in their lives. Some grow up in an abusive home while others live in neighborhoods where crime and other dangers are present.

Gun violence especially affects adolescents. It is now the leading cause of death among U.S. youth, overtaking car accidents.[14] More than half of the U.S. homicides in 2020 occurred among young people ages fifteen to thirty-four, according to the Centers for Disease Control and Prevention.

The impact of gun violence goes beyond just those directly involved. Whether it's the loss of a loved one, witnessing a shooting, or simply hearing gunshots in their neighborhood, children and teens are deeply affected. It takes a toll on their emotional and mental well-being and also their academic performance. Gun violence that becomes a norm in neighborhoods and schools impacts that generation and casts a shadow over the future of American youth.

This violence leaves teens feeling vulnerable, especially if while growing up they have not ever felt protected and taken care of by an adult. As a result, many teens end up carrying guns. Research has shown that teenagers who witness different types of violence are more likely to carry a firearm.[15] This perpetuates a cycle that makes these young people and those around them less safe.

Being surrounded by violence has an impact beyond a young person's physical and emotional well-being. When people are too afraid to take part in everyday behaviors, like sitting on their front steps, going for a walk, riding a bike, or visiting a local park, the social fabric disappears. It also affects the level of economic opportunity of their community. The resulting lack of investment deteriorates neighborhoods and increases crime, which leads to further disinvestment in housing, social services, retail, jobs, enrichment activities, and an overall uplifting environment that might otherwise help a young person excel.

Fear of getting killed or injured puts young people in a fight-or-flight mode, which makes it harder for them to learn, be emotionally stable, or practice their executive functioning. Safety is a basic need that enables young people to trust that they are secure and can pursue their interests and goals.

Technology
Maslow couldn't have imagined when he completed his pyramid in 1943 that technology would be where it is today. But as the last two decades have shown, technology is a newer but no less important basic need. In 2013, there were 2 billion cell phones and 1 billion users. In 2024, there were 7.2 billion cell phones and 4.8 billion users.[16]

While cell phones or internet access were once considered a luxury, most information and transactions are now online, making them a necessity. Everything from scheduling a doctor's appointment, checking in to see how your child is performing in class, applying for a job or benefits, or entering a public school lottery are all web-based activities. The COVID-19 pandemic accelerated this shift even further when online learning and more liberal work from home policies emerged.

Some 42 million Americans have no access to broadband, which provides high speed access to the internet.[17] Recent statistics show that nearly one-third of all low-income households do not have home internet service that they can access on a computer. Computers are vital for completing many job applications, job training programs, and classwork that are simply too complex to be done on a smartphone. Today, nearly all teens (97 percent) say they use the internet every day.[18] Young people's lives and future livelihood will suffer if they do not have access to the technology they need for school and work.

As we saw in Maslow's pyramid, we have not only these basic needs around health, food, housing, safety, and technology, but also psychological needs that are central and important for humans: belonging, relationships, a sense of purpose, and self-esteem.

Adolescents' developing brains are reward-fueled by dopamine and have lower inhibitions and a higher penchant for risk-taking, all while executive functioning, which would cause them to reflect or consider the impact of their actions, is still very much under construction.

Adolescents facing hunger could feel driven to steal food. Or they could enter into an unhealthy relationship if they see it as a pathway to stable housing. They may choose to carry a weapon to defend themselves. Or they might deny having a physical or mental health problem for fear of being perceived as different among the friend group whose approval they crave.

An added difficulty for teenagers who lack basic resources is that these circumstances stem from their family's challenges, over which they have no control. Meanwhile, young adults who are living on their own because of work, to attend college, or because they are parenting their own children are still developing the ability to navigate different resources, policies, and programs to meet their needs.

Lack of Basic Resources

While we have explored the impact on a young person of not having one of their essential needs met, the reality is that this deprivation typically extends to multiple needs. The best way to understand the scope of this is by measuring poverty, since limited income is what places many of life's necessities out of reach.

There was no clear or unified measure of poverty in the United States before the mid-1960s when President Lyndon B. Johnson pushed for federal officials to create a poverty baseline. The poverty thresholds were developed by the Social Security Administration based on an "economy food plan" created by the U.S. Department of Agriculture. In simple terms, it used the cost of a basic meal and assumed the average family spent about one-third of their budget on food. The cost was multiplied for larger family sizes.[19]

A few years later, the index for the poverty thresholds expanded from a government food plan to include the cost of food, gasoline/fuel, electricity, transportation, clothing, housing, and medical care—all of which make up the Consumer Price Index.

Four decades later, the U.S. Census Bureau continues to use this methodology to calculate the annual measure of the number of people living in poverty in the United States. The government takes this number and annually sets a "poverty line" that indicates the minimum amount of annual income that an individual or family needs to pay for essentials such as housing, utilities, clothing, food, and transportation.

The original poverty measurement was done in the 1960s and has only been adjusted for inflation since that time. Most experts agree that this is an underestimate of economic insecurity in modern American life.

These guidelines, or Federal Poverty Level (FPL), are based on the size of a household and the state where someone lives. In all but Alaska and Hawaii (due to the higher cost of living in those noncontiguous states), a family of four with annual earnings below $32,150 is considered poor in 2025. The federal Health and Human Services agency updates the poverty guidelines each year in January to account for inflation.

The data on how many people in the United States fall under

this line, especially children, shows that the problem affects millions of children today.

In 2020, 37.2 million people in the United States were living in poverty, or about 11.4 percent of the population—3.3 million more than 2019. About 16 percent of all U.S. children under age eighteen were living in poverty in 2020.[20] For adolescents specifically, about 1 in 7, or 13.3 percent, were living in families with incomes below the federal poverty line, defined as an income of $25,750 or less for a family of four in 2019.[21]

As you read those numbers, the problem might seem insurmountable. But policies can make a significant difference in the number of children living in poverty. In 2021, the U.S. Census Bureau reported that the number of children in poverty decreased by nearly half due to a temporary pandemic-related expansion of the child tax credit. However, when the expanded tax credit was not extended by Congress, the number of children in poverty increased. (In Part III, I will talk more about potential solutions that make a difference in the lives of adolescents.)

A suite of government programs exists to help those living below or close to the poverty line meet their basic needs. These programs make up what we typically refer to as the "safety net." They include, but are not limited to, the following:

- Health insurance through the Medicaid program
- Supplemental Nutrition Assistance Program (SNAP), which is often referred to as food stamps
- Temporary Assistance for Needy Families (TANF), which is cash assistance
- Childcare subsidies
- Housing vouchers
- Programs for expecting and new mothers called Special Supplemental Nutrition Program for Women, Infants, and Children (often called WIC)

- Support for people with disabilities who are unable to work

Federal poverty guidelines are mentioned most frequently in determining eligibility for one or more of these government assistance programs. Help is often available for more people than those officially below the poverty level. Many programs support those up to 150 percent or 185 percent of the poverty level, and the numbers vary by program and state, which can make all of it feel like a trick math question. One would assume it would be easy to tell if you qualify, but most programs are administered at the state and local levels and each program and jurisdiction has different criteria. It's not easy at all.

While millions of people are enrolled in these programs to help meet their basic needs, these programs have never been available to everyone who needs them due to funding limits. Many others may not know that they qualify and don't apply. Many others who do qualify have difficulty navigating the application process. That means that only a fraction of the people who need help are receiving it. The consequence: Millions of poor adolescents show up to the bridge to adulthood ill-equipped to cross because they don't have the essentials for their journey.

Although poverty is an important measure for all the reasons outlined, many more families are struggling. They earn income above the poverty level but can't make ends meet and are just scraping by. For many years, researchers and advocates have attempted to better understand the challenges that this group of families face. One recent example is the ALICE Essentials Index (ALICE is an acronym for Asset Limited, Income Constrained, Employed) developed by the United Way of Northern New Jersey.[22]

Stephanie Hoopes, a social entrepreneur and researcher, created the ALICE index. The project began when she was trying to document and explain the demand for social services in the New Jersey town where she lives among a group of people whose incomes exceeded the government's definition of poverty, but who still needed help. That research expanded to the state of New Jersey and then to twenty-seven states. As a result, Hoopes now runs the research and innovation center called United for ALICE at the United Way of Northern New Jersey.

The ALICE index takes a broader look at poverty with what it calls the Household Survival Budget: the minimum costs of household necessities including housing, childcare, food, transportation, health care, technology (a basic smartphone plan), and taxes, adjusted for household sizes and locations. The ALICE threshold is the minimum income required to afford the Household Survival Budget.

Armed with the ALICE threshold, it becomes apparent that official measures continue to undercount the number of U.S. households in financial hardship. According to the FPL, 13 percent of U.S. households (16.2 million) were in poverty in 2021. Yet United for ALICE data show that a different set of U.S. households, 29 percent (or 36.3 million), were ALICE.[23] ALICE households earn above the FPL, but not enough to afford the basics in the communities where they live.

Taken together, these data show that of the 130 million households in the United States in 2022, about 42 percent (55 million) had incomes below the ALICE Threshold of Financial Survival. The number of ALICE families has grown: In 2019, it was 50.4 million.

It is stunning to consider that almost half of American families struggle to meet their basic needs. This reality is in stark contrast to the notion of the United States as a land full of economic mobility and opportunity available to all.

A common belief is that two-parent households can avoid this fate. The data show that the two-parent family structure helps but does not guarantee financial stability. About 28 percent of children in households with two adults in the labor force were still below the 2019 ALICE threshold. There are dire implications for children growing up in families with income above the official poverty line but below a level of self-sufficiency. More than 23 million children below the ALICE threshold did not participate in SNAP and 11 million had no high-speed internet access at home.[24]

Hoopes discovered that there is a range of households that fall into the ALICE threshold, and they tend to be the individuals who keep the economy buzzing: coffee baristas, delivery drivers, home health aides, agricultural and childcare workers. This includes younger households—as in young adults in their first jobs trying to make a living—to older adults.

Because the government assistance programs are not based on a more realistic assessment of need, like the ALICE threshold, millions of families' needs go unmet.

Recent research from JUST Capital estimates that more than 50 percent of employees at the 1,000 biggest U.S. companies—roughly 11.1 million workers—aren't making enough to support a family of two adults and two children, even with one of those adults working full time.[25]

What's more, a GAO study found an estimated 5.7 million Medicaid enrollees and 4.7 million SNAP recipients in 2018 worked full-time hours.[26] This shows that struggling to make ends meet is not a function of not working hard enough. Rather, the reality is that millions of working people rely on public benefits to meet their basic needs.

Poverty determines what you eat, where you live, what kind of school you attend, and the quality of health care you receive. We are left, then, with adolescents growing up in families that grapple with the toxic stress (as described in Chapter 2) of maintaining a basic standard of living. All of these things can make the conditions of crossing the bridge of adolescence into adulthood much more difficult.

Researchers have found that chronic stress from poverty can

affect the brain, especially children's brain development. For example, in the period from birth to age three, when critical early brain development occurs, researchers conducting the Baby's First Years study have found a link between alleviating poverty and brain development. It showed that alleviating financial stress by providing poor mothers with a monthly cash stipend for the first year of their baby's life appeared to change the baby's brain activity and support cognitive development. Without proper early brain development, a child enters adolescence without a strong foundation, meaning their potential and future growth can be limited.[27]

In adolescence, material deprivation from poverty is similarly problematic. The adolescent brain is in a sensitive developmental period; young people need care and support to manage the many physical and emotional changes they are going through.

Parents who are working multiple jobs trying to make ends meet have less ability to focus on their adolescents' changing needs. Parental resilience and a parent's access to concrete support are two of the multiple factors that help keep a family safe and protected. This is significant for an adolescent because the combination of growing up in toxic stress (as I described in Part I) plus the lack of a supportive relationship with an adult can, over time, lead to negative changes, physically and emotionally.

Essentials like food, housing, and safety provide the stable foundation upon which adolescents build and grow their lives. Research, data, and the lived experiences of young people all point to the importance of having basic needs met. They are essential to the outcomes we want adolescents to accomplish and what they want for themselves.

Family plays an important role in meeting an adolescent's basic needs. And as we move up the pyramid of needs, family relationships for young people have another benefit to them: In the best circumstances, they fulfill an adolescent's psychological need for love, support, and belonging.

The people adolescents are connected to are guides who shape their experiences and steer them in their journey to adulthood. In the next chapter, I will describe just how important these bonds with adults are for adolescents and what can happen if they are fractured.

5

Permanent Connections

When you meet Sixto Cancel, what first strikes you is his quick enthusiasm. He believes that difficult problems can be solved. As the executive director and founder of Think of Us, he advocates for the lived experiences of foster children to be at the center of child welfare policy. He has given TED Talks, testified on Capitol Hill, and led Think of Us to use technology to build teen-first solutions that cater to the needs of youth in the foster care system.

To do all of this, he draws on his childhood and adolescence. He entered foster care at eleven months old. He and his siblings returned briefly to live with his mother when he was six, but her challenges and the lack of support to help her overcome them proved too great. He never returned home again.

At nine, he was adopted by a woman who kept a lock on her refrigerator and called him the N-word. He taped a recorder to his chest to gather the evidence to reverse his adoption and return to foster care. What should have been a reprieve ended up as continued difficulty. At thirteen, he landed in the home of an usher at his church who was eager to take care of him, but he struggled to connect to and trust her. He moved through different foster homes until he aged out of the child welfare system with no permanent family at twenty-three.

In his late twenties, Sixto met some of his father's extended family. He learned that four aunts and uncles had spent years raising children who were not their own. One aunt even helped raise his father, who died without ever meeting Sixto. That same aunt adopted four siblings and was a foster parent for thirty-five years.

Teeming with disbelief, Sixto pulled out his phone to check the distance between his aunt's house and where he grew up. It was 58 miles.

"That's how close I'd been to family members who would have taken me in, who I would have loved to live with. But the system never thought to find my family," Sixto says in his TED Talk.[1] Even as a young adult, Sixto wanted to and still felt a need to be connected to his family.

Every child, no matter the age, has a deep longing to be with their biological family and the sense of belonging they expect to find there. It is a basic human need to be accepted and fit in. And it is particularly important for teens given the neuroscience of the adolescent brain and the role of permanent connections during this developmental phase.

The adolescent brain undergoes extensive rewiring and is primed during adolescence to create healthy neural pathways based on the supportive connections they experience in relationships.

As we discussed in Chapter 1, the areas of the brain responsible for emotion are more sensitive during this period. That makes adolescents more attuned to their emotions and those of others. This opens up opportunities for adolescents to practice the development of skills, such as compassion and empathy, guided by and in relationships with caring adults:

Adults who listen to you.

Adults who want to get to know you.

Adults who see your potential.

Adults who help you recover from mistakes.

Adults who do not judge or try to "fix" you.

Adults who teach you the things that you do not yet know.

Adults who can coach you as you learn to make decisions for yourself.

Adolescents deserve to be in healthy relationships and loved by caring, supportive adults so they can feel like they are seen, are known for who they are, and are understood. There is a priceless richness to these caring relationships. They are the currency that a teen's everyday life is built upon and the well from which to draw when celebrating successes and navigating life's challenges. Love, belonging, and support have the power to change the trajectory of an adolescent's life. These kinds of connections are transformational, and they are vital for all young people on their journey to adulthood.

Adolescents benefit from multiple relationships that support their healthy passage into adulthood. But all young people need at least one. Usually, it comes from a family member—either a parent or another adult relative. In addition to or perhaps in place of family, a caring adult in the community, like a sports coach or teacher, may serve in this role. Someone who allows that young person to express their challenges and dreams, and who makes them feel comfortable enough to admit their mistakes and the things that embarrass them.

With this foundation of trust, these relationships must also challenge the young person in their actions. Without this aspect, the relationship may be pleasant but miss the opportunity to transform the young person's life by confronting them to do better when necessary and take on responsibility for the choices that create their life experience. I remember plenty of times letting Lauren know I wasn't pleased about something she said or did, and explaining why.

When the adult can show up without judgment for a young person, especially when they are facing a crisis, that also deepens the trust and helps build a transformational bond. That's because adolescence is a time of exploration, which usually includes making mistakes. A young person without a trusted, caring adult to rely on, when they make a mistake, is on their own to figure out how to manage challenges and the negative emotions that likely arise as a result. This is a tall order for their developing brains. Trying to navigate mistakes or adversity alone can lead to some of the toxic stress and trauma that I talked about in Chapter 2.

By contrast, when that adult shows up for them during times of crisis as a source of support, the young person feels safe and has an opportunity to grow through their mistake. They learn that there is an adult in their life they can turn to in their most vulnerable times.

Along each step of the way, adults need to show up as themselves in the relationship—express vulnerability and share times when they made mistakes—so that the emotional experience is not one-sided. Doing so allows the young person to practice empathy for adults. Also, if the youth and adult find shared interests or have gone through similar things—like a youth with experience in the juvenile justice system learning that their trusted adult has had a similar experience—it opens up multiple points of potential connection.

These behaviors—listening, spending time, challenging, showing up in crisis, and being real—are the ingredients to create a transformational relationship that is an essential emotional foundation for an adolescent's journey to adulthood. Ideally, these bonds are positive deposits of support into a young person and serve as pillars to their physical and emotional well-being. They offer guidance, nurturing, and a sense of belonging that is vital for how adolescents grow and develop into adulthood. These relationships help guide young people through the ups and downs of school, work, finances, and life issues.

Brain science is clear that when adolescents have secure attachments to adults, they can maximize the window of opportunity for brain development and the growth of the frontal lobe where all executive functioning happens. No matter what circumstance or living situation young people find themselves in, their brains crave loving, supportive connections.

However, for too many adolescents, the challenges they face make it more difficult for them to experience the benefits that come from transformational relationships.

As noted in Chapter 2, we should be particularly concerned about young people who become involved with child welfare or juvenile justice systems, where these connections are often fractured or never existed in the first place. Transformational relationships take on an even larger importance in the lives of young people who are facing difficult life circumstances.

Child Welfare

The relationships within families have the power to transform a young person's life, but sometimes families have issues that require outside intervention. Also known as child protection, child welfare is a system of services, policies, and interventions to ensure that children can lead healthy and safe lives.

With the priorities of child well-being, safety, and permanence, child welfare systems typically perform the following functions:

- Receive and investigate reports of possible child abuse and neglect
- Provide services to families that need assistance in the safety and care of their children
- Arrange for children to live with relatives or with foster families when they are not safe at home
- Arrange for reunification, adoption, or other permanent family connections for children and youth leaving foster care

Using the power to remove a child from their family is such a consequential decision. It abruptly interrupts and jeopardizes the ability of that child to have or develop the transformational relationship with their parents or caregivers that we know they will need. If their family's challenges are not resolved, the system is supposed to identify a permanent new family for the child or teen through legal guardianship with a family member—an arrangement called kinship care—or adoption.

Unfortunately for many older youth and teens ages fourteen to twenty-one, a permanent connection does not happen, leaving kids like Sixto adrift. Nearly 400,000 children were living in foster care in 2021, according to the most recent data from the Adoption and Foster Care Analysis and Reporting System. This is a decrease from four years prior, when the number was roughly 436,000.[2] However, children continually enter and exit the system, so the total number of children who came into contact in some way within the same year in the foster care system was more than 600,000.

The data further show that a majority of children (63 percent) are removed from their homes due to a finding of "neglect." By comparison, 36 percent of children were removed from their homes because of parental drug abuse. Children experiencing physical abuse made up 12 percent of those removed, and sexual abuse was the cause for 4 percent.[3]

Although a finding of neglect is the reason most children are removed from their homes and placed into foster care, there is no standard definition across the states or federal law for what constitutes neglect. Most often, it is defined as the failure to provide a child with needed food, clothing, shelter, medical care, or supervision.

Poor families are more likely to struggle to provide basic needs to their children, and that poverty could sometimes be reported as neglect. Supervision might be lacking if parents are working multiple jobs and different shifts trying to make ends meet. Forcefully removing a child from their home is a traumatic event and disrupts their family bonds. This most drastic of interventions should be limited to situations when it is necessary—not because a refrigerator is empty, there is no heat, or a teen is not getting along with his family. These are circumstances that can be remedied with the right resources or by addressing parent/child discord, all of which would cost far less than foster care. States spend more than $31 billion on child welfare services each year.[4]

Therefore, one of the best ways to ensure adolescents and young adults have permanent connections is to strengthen families. Rather than removing children from families, leaders must focus on addressing issues of poverty. If we ensure families can meet their basic needs (as discussed in the prior chapter), most of these kids would not go into foster care in the first place and could remain with their families without enduring the trauma of removal.

While neglect is a significant issue for younger children, older youth often come into foster care because of family conflict. Child behavior is listed as the cause for 11 percent of child removals involving youth older than twelve.[5]

Many factors lead adolescents into foster care because of behavior. Young adults may have experienced unaddressed trauma, and it is expressed in how they act. The young person may have lacked guidance in learning how to manage their emotions before adolescence, and the changing emotions of adolescence make this process more difficult. Families may simply lack the skills to communicate with each other and work through challenges in their relationships.

The right policies and programs can keep this type of conflict from tearing families apart. Community-based programs offer solutions and interventions to strengthen the family unit and prevent youth from going into foster care.

One such program founded in Canada, called Connect, is expanding in the United States. Connect trains certified facilitators who work with families throughout ten weeks in group sessions. Together they learn about adolescent development and effective ways to respond to youth behavior and emotions.

The difference this knowledge makes is dramatic. Caregivers

participating in the program reported feeling more hopeful and becoming a more effective guide for their young person. Meanwhile, youth in the program said they experienced fewer struggles with their behavior and in how they managed situations.[6] The program has been given the highest rating available by the California Evidence-Based Clearinghouse for Child Welfare: "Well-supported by research evidence."

A solution like Connect shows that something can be done to address these long-standing child welfare issues. I will talk more about solutions for adolescents and child welfare in Part III.

Although high-quality intervention programs like Connect are happening around the country, for multiple reasons, children will continue to be removed from their homes and placed into foster care. Some of those foster homes include people they don't know, and some of the foster homes are what is known as kinship care, when children are placed with relatives. Children and adolescents living in foster care deserve a safe and permanent family as they mature into adulthood if they can't be with their biological one.

In the case of children who are outside of their family's care, this kind of permanence could come through adoption or guardianship, in which the child receives emotional, social, financial, and other support from a person who is legally deemed to be their caregiving adult.

Another promising option for creating necessary permanence beyond reunification, adoption, and guardianship, particularly for older youth, is the SOUL Family Legal Permanency option. (SOUL stands for Support, Opportunity, Unity, Legal relationships.) Youth in foster care designed this approach to legal permanence. After piloting the approach in 2024, Kansas legislators passed a law formally installing SOUL Family, and another pilot is underway in Washington, D.C. The goal is to ensure that fewer adolescents leave foster care without a family or network of individuals who are committed to caring for and guiding them.[7]

This novel approach allows young people ages sixteen and older to establish a legal bond with one or more primary adults who will be there for them while keeping their family connections intact. It allows for the legal recognition of additional relationships in a young person's life with a broader network of caring adults. And it's not just about legalities—it means the young person will have access to vital benefits and services to support them on their journey to adulthood and beyond.

Failing to ensure young people in child welfare have permanent connections has far more than just psychological consequences; there is a threat of real bodily harm. For example, children who've experienced abuse and trauma, especially those in foster care or similar situations, are more likely to be targeted by sex traffickers.

It's hard to know exactly how many trafficked people have been in foster care, but studies show a strong connection. In 2021, for example, about 19 percent of missing kids from foster care were reported to have been trafficked for sex.[8] This shows we need to do more to protect kids in foster care and similar situations from being exploited. There is more we can and should do to ensure young people in child welfare have the permanent relationships they need to avoid these threats to their well-being.

Juvenile Justice

Some adolescents make decisions that get them into legal trouble. The juvenile justice system is a special legal framework for handling cases of children and adolescents who have committed offenses or engaged in delinquent behavior. It is separate from the adult criminal system and is supposed to focus on rehabilitation and treatment for young people instead of punishment.

While rehabilitation may be the goal, more often than not, juvenile justice becomes another system that removes children from their families, reduces their permanent connections, and disrupts their transformational relationships—the very things needed to help them heal and make different choices.

Justice-involved youth can often be the most overlooked. They are locked away, literally out of sight and too often out of mind, by society and sometimes even by the families they come from.

Adolescent brain science tells us that the neurons in young brains connect, refine, and learn based on experiences and relationships. When a young person is confined to a cell, that kind of developmental growth is tremendously curtailed.

I want to acknowledge that youth who are involved in the juvenile justice system have gotten off track in a way that has legal consequences. But when this happens, it is even more important for that young person to feel a sense of belonging with a caring adult. That kind of transformational relationship could help them learn from their mistakes, consider the consequences of their behavior, and pursue ways to make amends.

The supposed rehabilitative orientation of the juvenile justice system is why it is separate from the adult justice system. However, it can be easy for the justice system to overlook an adolescent's strengths and potential as an individual. Instead, there is more focus on their offense and little to no attention given to preventing or helping them heal from the situations and circumstances these young people have experienced. Such narrow thinking on the part of policymakers and leaders keeps young people disconnected from relationships and opportunities, and it limits their promise.

Engaging families is an important part of changing this dynamic. The family a justice-involved youth comes from has a powerful role to play if they are given a seat at the table while their young person is going through the juvenile justice process. That's because, at a time when the system is judging a young person for the worst thing they have done, their families know them more fully and can remind them of the dreams and hopes that they and their families have for their lives.

Unfortunately, many adolescents must navigate parts of this experience without the support and encouragement of their families because the system doesn't create many ways for families to have meaningful input. Yet, research shows that a family's involvement can make a positive contribution toward getting the young person back on track.[9]

Actively involving a family while their child is in the juvenile justice system is known as family engagement. It includes inviting parents to case planning meetings and seeking input on what works for their child. It can be a useful and important aid throughout the process of a young person's experience in the juvenile justice system.

In practice, family engagement means creating resources and opportunities for families to understand the juvenile justice process. It means ensuring families can participate in all key decisions regarding their child and can give their input on their child's strengths. Families also need an advocate to support them through the juvenile justice system, and someone to help them manage any feelings of shame, guilt, or fault because of the young person's choices.

Family engagement has the potential to create a meaningful partnership with families and youth at every level of the agency and throughout the system. This kind of partnership between families and system officials gives young people a stronger foundation of support and a better position to succeed after their justice involvement ends and they transition back into their home and community.

Family engagement takes planning, and there are a few characteristics that ensure it is successful. First, the concept of family engagement must include a mindset that all families have strengths, instead of the typical assumption that the child must have learned negative behaviors at home.

Also, systems must have a broader definition of family to include grandparents, cousins, aunts, uncles, and siblings—not just parents. Each family member has a unique relationship with the youth and holds a history and experiences that are significant to the young person who is involved in the juvenile justice system.

Also, reflecting and respecting family cultures and context are key. The stories, experiences, and culture that a young person comes from hold clues to their strengths and abilities. It can be easy for system officials to overlook this due to ignorance, assumptions, or bias.

Finally, it is important to allow adequate time for families and system personnel to build a trusting relationship.

The changes in the adolescent brain, and a deeper understanding of what is happening in a young person's development, can inform how we as a society respond to delinquent behavior. We know that young people respond more to rewards than punishment during this stage. Rather than working against these realities, we can use knowledge of brain science to shape policies and practices for how youth are treated in the juvenile justice system to help achieve better outcomes.

For example, brain science principles are leading some juvenile justice systems to transform their approach to youth probation. Probation is an important area of reform in juvenile justice because it is the sanction used in the majority of juvenile court cases. According to the U.S. Department of Justice, of the 722,600 delinquency cases in 2019, about 53 percent, or approximately 203,600 cases, were adjudicated or resolved with a judge finding a young person guilty of committing a delinquent act and placing them on probation.[10] That same year, an estimated 52,000 cases in the system that did not end up in court also resulted in young people being placed on probation.[11]

Right now, most jurisdictions use a surveillance-based approach to probation with conditions. Typically, young people are given a long list of rules to follow—like regular meetings with a probation officer, adhering to a curfew, engaging in work or school, or completing a specified number of community service hours.

These all sound like necessary and reasonable structures designed to change a young person for the better, but this approach is not aligned with their brain development at this stage. Since risk-taking and disobeying rules are common and developmentally expected from adolescents, probation officers are put into a position of surveillance and monitoring, not rehabilitation. As we have explored throughout this book, the young person needs to have key relationships and support, plus learn to tap into positive motivations to make different choices. Rote compliance does not get them there, given the realities of the adolescent brain.

When the whole system is set up to focus on and record how many mistakes or probation violations a young person makes, the arrangement does not position them for success or even align with their level of maturity.

Therefore, traditional probation often unfolds like this: At its best, it allows court-involved juveniles to remain in their community and be connected to constructive and therapeutic activities rather than be incarcerated. However, a risk-taking adolescent may frustrate authorities with their behavior that breaks probation rules. Then, even if the young person poses no threat to public safety, they could be incarcerated because of their noncompliance. The result: young people going deeper into the system rather than rebounding from their errors. For example, a 2015 U.S. Department of Justice report showed that in eight states, the number of young people in custody for technical violations of parole was larger than the number of young people who had committed an offense on another person.[12] In other words, they were locked up not because they broke the law but because they broke the rules of probation.

There is no evidence to support the idea that probation practices that rely on lengthy court conditions and compliance-oriented practices are successful in improving youth behavior. Recent research led by Naomi Goldstein of Drexel University found that most juvenile probation systems are designed in a way that misses the opportunity to acknowledge and take advantage of adolescent development.

That's because juvenile probation typically mirrors adult probation, in effect negating the approach and desire to treat youth offenders differently by having them go through a juvenile system. Instead, the juvenile court process typically leads to a situation where, like adults, if a young person fails to comply with probation rules, they face harsh consequences. This is even as the Supreme Court has found in several of their rulings that an adolescent's immaturity deserves special legal protection.[13]

However, there is a different way.

Goldstein's research found that some juvenile justice systems around the country are reforming their approach to probation with dramatically different results. These efforts use strategies that are aligned with adolescent brain science. By focusing on reward and incentive-based strategies, the system can motivate youth to meet more positively framed requirements.

This approach is known as an incentive-based model. Think of it as the difference between communicating to a young person about their efforts, "You're on the right track!" vs. "You're wrong!" It takes advantage of an adolescent's motivation and their brain's responsiveness to rewards at this stage of development. Incentive-based models help adolescents learn and implement new, desired behaviors instead of being punished for breaking a rule.

One example is a program called Opportunity-Based Probation in Tacoma, Washington. It was designed in partnership with Sarah Walker, a research associate professor at the University of Washington. The program design is rooted in research showing that based on the adolescent brain, youth respond better to rewards and incentives for positive behavior than to the threat of punishment.[14]

It works this way: Probation staff, young people, and their caregivers collaborate to develop a case plan and define weekly goals. Positive behaviors and met milestones earn participating youth points, which they can redeem for rewards (such as movie theater tickets) or enrichment activities in the community (i.e., a job shadowing opportunity). When the young person reaches certain benchmarks, they can have fewer supervision meetings and ultimately earn early release from probation.[15]

An eighteen-month evaluation of the first phase of the program compared youth who were enrolled in Opportunity-Based Probation versus traditional monitoring. Participants in the incentive-based approach logged 60 percent fewer new referrals to court and 67 percent fewer probation violations compared to their traditionally supported peers. Also, 53 percent of the participants in the study were young people of color.[16] This indicates that incentive-based approaches may be a promising option for reducing the disproportionate number of young people of color involved in the juvenile justice system.

Innovative and brain-based practices geared to adolescents in the juvenile justice system like incentive-based probation help ensure that young people remain with their families and can benefit from the love, support, and guidance this provides, rather than the isolation and emotional disconnection of incarceration.

Mentoring

An area of research called positive youth development looks at all the ways that young people can grow up healthy by focusing on their strengths instead of just their shortcomings. Positive youth development research has shown time and again the importance of nurturing connections with caring adults who serve as role models. Sadly, many young people today still lack these supportive relationships.

That's where mentoring comes in. Mentoring pairs young people, or mentees, with responsible and caring mentors, usually adults. It's become an increasingly popular strategy to build on youths' strengths and provide needed support.

Mentoring works because it creates a special bond between the mentor and mentee. Mentors, who often have more life experience, offer guidance, perspective, and opportunities to help young people thrive and reach their goals. Whether formal or informal, mentoring relationships are built on empathy, consistency, and lasting connections. Mentors serve as role models, teachers, and advisors, providing the kind of support that can make a real difference in a young person's life.

While mentoring relationships have become more common in the last thirty years, data show a decline in the prevalence of mentoring. A 2023 national study led by the organization MENTOR found that the share of youth ages eighteen to twenty-one who report having had a mentor while growing up dropped 6 percentage points over the past decade, from 66 percent in 2013 to 60 percent in 2022. Reports of having a naturally occurring mentor, rather than a program-provided one, dropped by 13 percentage points. More than 1 in 3 (35 percent) young adults say they grew up without the support of any mentor.[17]

There is certainly a need to reverse this trend. I raise this because all youth—whether involved in the juvenile justice system or not—can benefit from the positive support of a mentor.

One of the most powerful mentoring programs I've seen is run by Thread, a program based in Baltimore. Thread connects students, university- and community-based volunteers, and collaborators to provide practical and emotional wraparound services for youth who need them.

Thread seeks out ninth-grade students facing tough challenges, especially those at risk of not graduating from high school—such as those in the bottom 25 percent of their class. Each student is matched with a group of up to four volunteers, creating a diverse support network that feels like family. Together, they tackle everything from academic struggles to everyday needs like transportation and meals.

Thread doesn't just offer short-term help—it's a commitment that lasts for ten years, seeing students through high school and beyond. The program creates powerful results for the students in it:[18]

- 77 percent of students graduate from high school, defying the odds stacked against them.
- Every single student stays enrolled in Thread for the full ten years, no matter what challenges they face.
- More than half—57 percent—of Thread alumni have gone on to complete a postsecondary degree or certificate program, setting them up for success in the future.

Thread isn't just a program but a lifeline for young people that provides the support and guidance they need to thrive despite the obstacles they face. That is the power of relationships. I'll talk more about Thread in Chapter 12.

After a young person's urgent physical needs are met, trusted and caring relationships with adults are the emotional infrastructure that sustains them on the journey to adulthood, no matter their circumstances—whether sitting in juvenile confinement awaiting a trial, hoping for an adoption to be finalized, or living with their biological family. With this kind of emotional foundation, a young person is ready to take steps toward the opportunities that will help them realize their personal goals.

The most immediate ambition most teens have is to complete high school and perhaps pursue postsecondary education, a critical marker for readiness for adulthood. In the next chapter, I will talk about the importance of education in setting up adolescents for life success.

6

Education and Credentials

Nicole Lynn Lewis always knew she would graduate from high school and go to college. Her two college-educated parents stressed higher education to her and her sister as they grew up. For years she worked hard in her classes in anticipation of going to college. By the time she got to senior year, Nicole was a self-described "rock star" student, applying to different colleges and ready to make her post–high school dreams come true.

Months before graduation, the acceptance letters started rolling in. Nicole read each one, holding it above her soon-to-be bulging belly.

Nicole was pregnant.

She was at the end of her senior year when she found out she would be a mother. She was shocked, devastated, and scared. She was afraid that everything her parents had prepared her for, and that she had worked so hard for, had evaporated. As she tried to process her feelings, she found that the same adults around her who had been championing her road to college were now convinced her life was forever doomed.

Nicole could feel her emotional support eroding. She tried to steer herself through the new reality of graduating from high school and getting to college while being a mother. Help came from her high school principal, who made sure that Nicole had the support she needed. But even with that support, she knew she needed more time to make the transition to college.

She took a year off after graduation and tried to make things work with the father of her daughter. But that proved challenging and she experienced homelessness while navigating their difficult relationship.[1] Despite these barriers, Nicole reopened her college applications and enrolled at the College of William and Mary when her daughter was three months old.

"I knew that my education was probably the best way for me to provide for this baby, but I didn't have a path to get there," she told me when I interviewed her for our Casey podcast. "It was a really scary time."[2]

Nicole graduated successfully—a feat given that nationally fewer than 2 percent of new mothers earn a bachelor's degree by age thirty. And she described the grit and grace it took to do so in her book *Pregnant Girl*. She wanted to do more for others in a similar situation and created a nonprofit, Generation Hope, to support other young parents going through college.[3]

For Nicole and millions of other students, the importance of graduating from high school no matter the obstacles cannot be overstated. It is a crucial milestone, an important foundation for a healthy and successful adulthood, and a core building block in a young person's life.

Education helps young people develop knowledge, build relationships with peers and adults, and identify their values and preferences. It helps them develop the cognitive, interpersonal, and executive functioning skills they need to navigate their future. As young people pursue their education during adolescence, their learning is a time to try out new ideas and experiences in a supportive setting with adults.

Educational opportunities also give young people the ability to think abstractly, increase their reasoning, practice considering multiple points of view, and the ability to solve complex problems and relate to others.

High school graduation is critical because, on average, high school graduates have better job opportunities and higher earning potential compared to individuals without a diploma. According to the U.S. Bureau of Labor Statistics, high school graduates have a significantly lower unemployment rate compared to those who did not complete high school. Between October 2021 and October 2022, 538,000 young people dropped out of high school. The labor force participation rate for recent dropouts during that same period, 41.9 percent, was much lower than the rate for recent high school graduates not enrolled in college, 69.2 percent.[4]

These statistics show a strong correlation between high school educational attainment and employment prospects. A high school diploma is required for most jobs. High school graduates have higher average incomes over their lifetimes than nongraduates, so the credential has a significant impact on the likelihood of future poverty.

Research also shows a relationship between high school graduation and physical health. As long as health care and medical coverage remain tied to employer-sponsored health coverage, high school graduates who go on to have higher rates of employment tend to be healthier because of access to health coverage.[5] Additionally, studies show that adults with higher levels of education are less likely to engage in risky behaviors such as drinking or smoking. More years of education are correlated with young people growing into adults with the knowledge and tools to make healthier choices.

One of the most obvious benefits of high school graduation for adolescents is that it opens the door to further educational opportunities such as college or vocational training. Adolescents who graduate from high school are more likely to pursue higher education, leading to expanded career options and increased earning potential.

Depending on a family's history of high school completion, high school graduates can also shape and set positive examples for their families and future generations. As they grow into adulthood and become parents themselves, they are likely to prioritize their children's education.

Adolescents have better health, wealth, and career prospects and outcomes when they graduate from high school on their journey to adulthood. They set themselves up for economic stability, and the knowledge and interest to engage in society in new and meaningful ways. The social benefits of graduating from high school include a sense of personal achievement and satisfaction, and the power to inspire and help create a brighter future for individuals and their families.

High school graduation is also an achievement that a young person can accomplish only by taking ownership of and participating in their education. No one else can do it for them. At this juncture of adolescence, high school becomes the point when a young person learns to be responsible for completing assignments, being diligent about studying, and figuring out what they might want to do in the next phase of their life. To create possibilities and options for their lives as they grow into adulthood, young people need a clear path to high school graduation.

Education has seen many shifts in recent decades, including what students learn; how they learn; and where they learn. Still, education remains the most powerful pathway enabling young people to achieve credentials that become valuable assets—opening up opportunities, helping them get on a career path, and supporting financial stability and self-sufficiency.

In many places, high school graduation seems woven into the fabric of community expectations. The milestone is assumed and nearly taken for granted: Of course, local students will complete high school. In other places, high school graduation is anything but expected. Long before graduation day, students drop out for lack of engagement or to earn income in support of their families, are placed in juvenile facilities for committing a crime, lose their lives to community violence, live away from their original families in foster care, or suffer so much lost school time that they don't have enough credits to qualify for graduation.

Education and Credentials

In the 2021–22 school year, the U.S. graduation rate was 87 percent.[6] That represents the rate of public school students who enter ninth grade and graduate within four years with a regular diploma, according to data from the National Center for Education Statistics (NCES).[7] As I described in Chapter 2, some adolescents face steeper odds based on the traumas and experiences they have been through. When you break down graduation statistics by different groups of young people, you can see differences and opportunity gaps.

As a group, according to NCES, Asian and Pacific Islander young people have the highest U.S. graduation rate. They complete high school at a rate of 93 percent, followed by white students (90 percent), Hispanic students (83 percent), Black students (81 percent), and American Indian or Alaska Native (75 percent).

For youth who are in foster care, graduating from high school can be a challenge. The graduation rate for students in foster care was 65 percent, compared to 86 percent among all youth ages eighteen to twenty-four.[8]

Juvenile incarceration (even for short periods) also affects high school graduation. The reasons why go beyond the government systems these young people are in. Young people in foster care or involved in juvenile justice often must overcome greater barriers to graduation due to poverty, lower-performing schools, disruptive school changes, and unsafe neighborhoods. But juvenile justice and child welfare systems have an important responsibility to prepare the young people in their care for this milestone, and the graduation rates show our systems can and must do better.

We need more innovative solutions so all adolescents reach high school completion. We know from adolescent brain science that young people at this stage value relationships and learning through experiences. They need positive environments for their brains to develop and grow and they need to be part of a supportive learning environment that has high expectations. The good news is that an increasing number of promising options are emerging.

Education Models

I remember when my daughter entered high school. The hope and expectation were that she would get through the next four years and successfully graduate. Today, that is still largely the expectation: Young people will move forward with a course of study over four years, then consider college. On the one hand, this gives students a clear goal and a timeline for getting there. However, the graduation data I shared earlier show that this linear approach doesn't work for all students.

While sit-and-learn may be the predominant educational model, we have evidence from dropout rates that traditional education pathways do not work for all young people. For many, the transition to young adulthood comes with additional family responsibilities that do not align with inflexible traditional school models.

We often see that many low-income young adults and young adults of color must work to financially contribute to their households. In some instances, a young person—like Nicole—is a parent and must support their family. This additional responsibility can affect their ability to make educational decisions.

Some of the young people who do not earn a high school diploma within four years have experienced major adversity, including poverty, abuse, or neglect. I discussed in Chapter 2 how toxic stress that is generated by adversity can change the developing adolescent brain and affect outcomes like education. It is possible to adopt more flexible education strategies designed to meet the needs of young people whose brains are affected by trauma or face other challenges that put them at high risk of dropping out of school. Those students have strengths and potential that need to be cultivated differently, and a modified education program could help them discover and grow those strengths.

Flexible School Models

In my role at Casey, I have spoken directly to many young people from different backgrounds and experiences and listened to them describe what they want for their lives. They have said many things in common when it comes to education. In particular, they want to meaningfully connect with adults and take part in environments where they feel like they belong. School is where they spend most of their time away from home and young people say that they want an educational experience that reflects what they feel they need to thrive as students.

Students are calling for something different with regard to their education. And the data show that not all students are engaged when it comes to starting and completing high school. That means there is an opportunity for alternative models that would engage students and help them complete their high school education.

There is some confusion about what that term "alternative" even means, according to a report by Education Northwest that looked at high school alternatives across the country.[9] In defining what a high school alternative is, the report acknowledges some of the stereotypes around the term. Does it signal that these students have failed in traditional settings? Are these schools vibrant places of learning or simply warehouses where no real learning takes place? Have the students in these alternative schools been pushed out?

On the contrary, the report finds that alternative schools can embody a welcoming environment that includes some of the following elements:

- High expectations for all students, built around supporting a student's strengths to boost their confidence in their ability
- Strong adult-student relationships

- Alternative accountability measures, since academic results on tests often don't reflect student engagement or academic growth
- Comprehensive services that include making sure their basic needs are met, plus emotional support
- Extra academic support [10]
- Engaging curriculum and a stimulating environment (high school students who consider dropping out say lack of engagement is the primary reason)[11]

One example of an organization providing this kind of opportunity is the Goodwill Excel Center, a national public school model that holds eight-week terms year-round to support anyone who has completed eighth grade in receiving their high school diplomas. It also provides services like on-site childcare.

David Ramirez, an Excel student, started high school in Indianapolis and was doing well in his classes. He had a goal of becoming an athlete. But he started hanging out with friends who didn't value school, he missed his sports practices, and he was arrested and expelled from high school. He ended up getting detained in a juvenile facility.

After he was released, he wanted to get back on track. He was on probation and, at age eighteen, couldn't find a traditional school that would accept him. Then he enrolled in the Goodwill program. The Excel Center provided support, such as a coach who helped him get to school when he had no reliable source of transportation. He graduated in a year and was hired as a mechanic after earning a craftsmanship certificate at the school. He has plans to enroll in college.

David said, "I didn't know that they would be so helpful, that they would actually be so involved in your life. I wouldn't have landed the job I have now or felt like I needed to start a career and actually earn a living without coming [to the Excel Center] and earning a high school diploma."[12]

Beyond High School

After high school, many young people have bold dreams and aspirations. They want to pursue higher education as a stepping stone to a well-paying job. Other students are motivated to improve their family's economic well-being through work or training programs. Some young people are also parents, so they need to ensure that they can provide for their children by achieving an industry-recognized credential.

Scan any online job board and you'll see that many jobs in the United States require a college degree or training beyond a high school diploma. A college degree is associated with many benefits. These include the ability to earn more, lower unemployment rates, higher average earnings, and better health.

While college enrollment rates appear to have rebounded from the lows we saw during the pandemic,[13] access to postsecondary education remains out of reach for millions of young people in the United States. Rising tuition and living expenses exceed financial aid, frequently requiring students to work and take out student loans. Many students, particularly low-income students, first-generation college enrollees, immigrants, working students, and student parents, struggle to persist and graduate.

At high-poverty high schools, about half of the students enrolled in college, according to 2022 data.[14] Starting, though, is insufficient. Students must persist—complete their freshman year and return. Experts measure this "persistence rate" to ensure college admission and entrance data tell a full picture of college completion.

First-year college students from high-poverty schools completed their freshman year at a rate of 72 percent in 2020. By contrast, the persistence rate for first-year college students from wealthier schools was much higher, 90 percent. In 2021, the number of students at low-poverty schools who even enrolled in college was 71 percent.

One important factor in college attendance and completion is cost, given that nearly half of all young people are growing up in families struggling to make ends meet. Young people of color face disproportionate barriers to college due to income, which translates to higher student loan debt. This creates a burdensome drag on their future financial stability.

Black college graduates owe an average of $25,000 more in student loan debt compared to white borrowers.[15] Four years after graduation, Black students owe an average of 88 percent more than white borrowers. African American student borrowers are the most likely to struggle financially due to student loan debt requiring monthly payments of $250 on average. It's clear that even if young people of color make it to college, they face hurdles in finishing their degrees and then repaying education loans.

To address these issues and support all young people through high school graduation, college completion, and beyond, it is critical for pathways to higher education and training to deploy more inclusive, tailored approaches so that more young people can stay connected. The Foundation's Learn and Earn to Achieve Potential, or LEAP™, demonstrated ways to address this challenge.

This initiative focused on creating educational and employment pathways for youth and young adults who are in foster care, involved in the criminal justice system, or homeless. Through local partnerships in ten states, the initiative demonstrated ways to help young people address the trauma they may have experienced in their lives and equip them to succeed in school and at work. It supported their education pursuits—a high school diploma or equivalency—and provided services to overcome the unique challenges they face and meet their basic needs.

Consider one community partner in the LEAP program, the

Coalition for Responsible Community Development. The Los Angeles–based coalition provides a range of education and job training programs for young people who have become disconnected or disengaged from school in Los Angeles County.

Young people without a high school diploma can join a program run by the Coalition, Jobs for Los Angeles Graduates. There, young people enroll in training programs that prepare them for careers in growing industries. Those who already have a high school diploma or equivalent can choose to attend Los Angeles Trade Technical College. The Coalition also works with the city's public schools to prevent dropouts and help youth who are at risk of getting involved in the criminal justice and other public systems.

The Coalition as a community partner provides young people in Los Angeles with paths to college or careers by working with many other partners, including organizations in child welfare, justice, homeless services, workforce development, public housing, and education. These partnerships help young people to more seamlessly navigate the systems they participate in and achieve their career and education goals. Comprehensive supportive services, authentic adult-youth relationships, and leadership development are key aspects of the LEAP design.

The education system has tremendous potential to capitalize on the strengths of young people by designing programs and experiences that help young people learn best. If learning environments are key for giving adolescents the skills they need for success, the workplace is the arena where young people can practice those skills. There are many challenges and opportunities young adults face when they start to enter the workforce. In the next chapter, I detail what happens and needs to happen when adolescents start working.

7

Financial Stability and Well-Being

It was another day on the job at a doctor's office for Esther Aidelemon. She had a clerical role and earned $9 an hour. The job offered stability and some income. But it didn't pay enough to make ends meet and there was no opportunity for growth. On the weekends, she drove Uber.

One day on a whim, she searched online for free technology training. Esther googled "free IT courses." This search led her to Per Scholas, a nonprofit that offers tuition-free IT training, financial guidance, and career coaching. She enrolled in their fifteen-week course that met eight hours a day, five days a week. Upon completion, she accepted a role as a senior IT specialist at a health care company. Per Scholas provided her with a financial coach who helped her set financial goals, create a budget, eliminate her personal debt, and negotiate her job offer.[1]

Esther now sees a future beyond her present circumstances. "As an IT professional, you always have to keep learning," she says. "You can't say, I'm just going to do this and that's it."[2]

Young people must master the skills of earning and managing money if they are to thrive into adulthood. Their journey toward financial mastery is about more than dollars and cents: It is the freedom to pursue their passions, achieve their dreams, and build a life of security and prosperity for themselves and those they care about. Learning how to earn money and manage it allows young people to practice their growing executive functioning skills and sets a strong foundation for their entire adulthood.

This starts with an adolescent's first job and the ones that follow. These early work experiences are an important rite of passage for young people. They may spend twelve to sixteen years or more in school but they work for the majority of their lives. They will need to make a transition from student to employee, and the process is not automatic. Employment gives young people the opportunity to grow their maturity while they earn income that makes the prospect of financial stability possible.

Navigating the New World of Work

Most of us can remember the feelings of independence and pride we experienced in our first paid job. At age fourteen, I was hired to be the children's choir director at my church for $100 a month. Later as a teenager, I had other jobs in retail and marketing. In college, I worked part time at a grocery store, a doctor's office, and the university's library. These were all important opportunities for me to learn how to take direction from supervisors, be dependable, pay taxes, start building credit, and learn to budget my money.

It is still important for young people to have early job experiences. But few things remain the same from the time I was born more than half a century ago, and the American labor force is no exception. Between 1969 and the present day, nearly every aspect of the country's workforce and workplace has changed.[3] The demographic makeup of who goes to work is radically different than it was fifty years ago, as is the type of work individuals do, how they do it, how they're paid, and even how they save for retirement. Certain industries like computer programming, coding, and alternative energy sectors were all but unimaginable half a century ago.

For young people, the process of entering the world of work is more complicated. Gone are the days of paper applications and plentiful coveted factory jobs. Instead, the rise in technology has meant applying to nearly all jobs online with higher-paying jobs often requiring more communication and analytical skills like working with data.[4] While manufacturing positions have declined, there has been an increase in service jobs and gig work powered by technology, like on-demand food delivery.

More data and the need for writing skills have created a growing number of middle- and upper-skill jobs with increased minimum job qualifications that often include a four-year degree. Hiring managers screen candidates for soft skills like collaboration and judgment—areas that are still in development for adolescents and young adults. Sadly, many entry-level positions do not provide pathways to greater economic opportunity, as Esther, the clerk in the doctor's office, experienced. So, even when they step into a first job, young people can find themselves stuck and needing to pivot.

All of this translates into a shift in the way that young people have to navigate their path to and beyond their first job. They need help sorting out what kinds of opportunities and work structures are right for them, how to obtain the necessary qualifications for those roles, and how to turn a job into a career.

Programs like Per Scholas are an example of the power of innovative approaches to support a young person's entry into the workforce or to make a career transition. Having a job with the potential for upward mobility is an important cornerstone of stability and opportunity that young people need.

Lots of young people are entering the workforce in both part-time and full-time roles. The youth labor force, ages sixteen to twenty-four, who are working or actively looking for work, grows between April and July, when larger numbers of high school and college students take on summer jobs, and college graduates look for full-time work. In July 2023, 55 percent of young people ages sixteen to twenty-four were employed, according to the U.S. Bureau of Labor Statistics.[5] As adults, our focus should be on making sure these experiences are positive and give them something to build upon.

Youth and young adults need meaningful work experiences and support in their early career roles as a way to obtain long-term economic stability so they can grow their workplace skills for the future. A young person's ability to find and keep meaningful work is more than an individual journey and responsibility. That's because new workers are the future generations that will drive our economy. Research has shown that for twenty-five- to thirty-four-year-olds working full time and year-round, the earnings for those who completed some postsecondary education was up to 59 percent higher than those who completed high school.[6] We need young people to succeed.

All these changes mean that we have to prepare young people to persist in a labor market and global business environment in a new way that may be unlike prior generations. Adolescent brain development affects and can inform how we help young people enter and grow in the workplace.

Work and the Adolescent Brain

The expectations of work, both technical and interpersonal, can be a challenging prospect for adolescents. Because of their developing brains, young people are still figuring out their identity and their interests. Without the benefit of strong executive functioning skills, it is often difficult for them to find their first job experience. Also, some higher-income youth benefit from the networks and connections of their family to help them get internships and first jobs.

For many young people, particularly those from low-income families or living in high-poverty neighborhoods, work isn't optional. It is a necessity to supply the financial resources so they can provide for themselves and their family. They might want or need to take jobs that pay more but provide fewer opportunities for career advancement. Other barriers may complicate their progress up the career ladder. There could be a mismatch between where people live and where the jobs are, making the search for employment difficult. Additionally, some employers may be hesitant to hire a younger employee.

Young people who are involved in the juvenile justice or child welfare system face unique barriers to work. They may be in group homes or correctional facilities that prohibit or limit their ability to pursue early work opportunities. They may be surrounded by adults who fail to see their potential and don't believe they could prosper in anything. As a result, they are denied access to work or start on this critical path far too late.

Research shows that the effectiveness of adolescent employment depends on the factors present in an adolescent's life before their first work opportunity.[7] For example, a thirty-two-year study covering three generations, known as the Youth Development Study, looked at the experiences of adolescents and tracked them into adulthood, including their parents and their eventual children. The researchers found that the choices youth and young adults make regarding work during high school are influenced by their social backgrounds and factors such as family circumstances and socioeconomic status. Also, a young person's motivations influence how they experience their early work opportunities.

As I described in Part I of this book, the executive functioning portions of the adolescent brain are still under development even into the early twenties. These younger brains are wired for reward and need to take risks to learn. They are also focused on relationships as an important source of support. But some of these aspects of a young person's development can make work a challenge because the business world thrives on efficiency, high expectations for execution, and little time for mentoring and nurturing new talent.

However, adolescents are in a period of developmental growth and brain plasticity, which means that they can take in new approaches and learn rapidly. Therefore, a trial-and-error approach to work is critically important in giving young people chances to understand their role, make mistakes, and learn from those mistakes—just like any new employee might. They aren't set in their ways and can quickly learn new skills with the right support.

With their evolving maturity, young people must strike a delicate balance as they navigate their early work experiences. Workplaces operate on thoughtful and clear communication (even if this is still an aspirational goal for some places). To meaningfully participate in work, a young person must communicate their thoughts and needs, work on a team, solve problems, manage their time, and be adaptable.

While young people are expected to demonstrate aspects of these skills in an educational setting, in the workplace they are expected to do so consistently and at a higher level—often amidst the shifting and unpredictable priorities of a workplace. They may start to gain these skills in school, but through work, they are expanded and refined. The experience that a young person has in learning how to acquire and demonstrate these kinds of interpersonal skills is valuable for their professional and personal development—and their future careers.

The difficulty is that many workplaces and work programs for young people can have expectations of know-how or assume competence and may not have the patience for a young person's kind of trial-and-error approach to the work. It is especially difficult for young adults who are new to working to have access to the opportunities that allow them to learn while also teaching them basic workplace skills.

Young people have always had some difficulty adapting to the workplace. But when most jobs were manual and few had technical components, it was easier for young people to adapt. Now, the widespread use of technology in nearly every role has made even basic jobs more complex, and I believe that has made it harder for young people to enter the workforce successfully. And shifting expectations will continue. According to a 2023 report from the World Economic Forum, 44 percent of workers' core skills are expected to change in the next five years.[8]

With adolescents and young adults in a dynamic developmental phase, the kind of work experiences and opportunities that are available to them need to be tailored to their developmental needs, both for the benefit of the young person and the employer. That means experiences and opportunities should take into account that young people are learning things for the first time, developing their identity, and growing their personal and professional skills so that they can contribute to the workforce.

Benefits of Youth Employment

Young people start to encounter what they might call the "real world" in the workplace. They work alongside adults who have job responsibilities, and the young person's ideas and effort make a contribution to meeting those responsibilities. Everyone in the workplace is on the same team, working toward organizational goals.

Early work experiences make a positive contribution to the lives of young people in multiple ways. Adolescent brain science shows that youth and young adults are especially motivated by rewards, so the monetary gain of employment is an important factor to get young people interested in early work experiences. Work allows young people to have financial resources so they can learn the fundamentals of personal finance in balancing earnings and income. This gives them a foundation of financial literacy. Work also allows adolescents and young adults to get knowledge, skills, and experience to begin to grow their careers. As they seek to advance, young people get to practice strategizing and planning their next professional move, which hopefully allows them to earn more. Finally, all these benefits of work for young people are best developed in the context of work relationships with trusted adults who will listen to their ideas, give them constructive feedback, provide guidance on financial matters, and help support them through all stages of the process.

Employment experiences for youth and young adults also help them explore and discover new things: different industries, multiple job roles, and contrasting work environments. This is the time when young people who get an early office job may discover that they like to work outside. Or they prefer working in a small company or startup operation compared to a large and established organization. Or they might want to become an entrepreneur after experiencing the structure of a 9 to 5 job. This kind of exposure to new experiences is essential for helping young people identify their interests, the kinds of environments where they flourish, and what kind of work they may prefer. This is an area where the adolescent brain and its wiring for being open to new experiences is a strength in the workplace and can help them choose a suitable career path.

Youth employment gives adolescents the experiences they need to put on their resumes so that they can qualify for future jobs. That credibility is built on several things: their commitment to a past employer, demonstrated work experience, and results in the workplace. Simply put, past work experience makes young people more employable.

Given the complexities we just explained about how to make work feasible for young people given their developmental stage, let me share some examples I have seen make a difference. There are three best practices in terms of youth and work that can foster the best early work experiences: apprenticeships, summer jobs programs, and social enterprises.

1. Apprenticeships

Amantha Hons grew up in a small town outside of San Antonio, Texas, and received her degree from Texas A&M University. After graduation, she did what many young people do; she looked for her first full-time job.

She wanted a role in her chosen field of marketing. As a twenty-two-year-old newly minted graduate, she had some work experience. But as she started her first job search, she found that the competition was stiff and employers were not impressed with her kind of work history—college internships and part-time jobs. She struggled to get hired into a full-time role.

Then, she found an apprenticeship program—one that offered paid training in the job-readiness skills she needed to become successful. It also taught her how to search for and land her first full-time role. In the program, she was able to experiment and find her way. Without the extra support, she said, "Who knows if I would have made it as far in my career as I have today?"[9]

Formal training programs like paid apprenticeships offer hands-on training, often in specific industries or professions. They are often used in industries like construction or electrical work. However, a variety of industries like education and health use apprenticeships as a way for participants to acquire the relevant skills required for their chosen careers. Formal work programs connect academic learning to the practical demands of the workplace.

The U.S. Department of Labor's Office of Apprenticeship, the Employment and Training Administration program that oversees registered apprenticeships, counted almost 600,000 active apprentices in nearly 27,000 registered apprenticeship programs in 2022.[10] Luckily this trend is growing as more employers in more industries utilize apprenticeships to access and develop talent for the future.

2. Summer Jobs

It is not unusual in the summer to see young people working in retail, restaurants, or manual labor jobs. Many youth work experiences come in the form of government-funded summer youth employment programs. They are typically run by workforce development agencies, youth development nonprofits, and educational institutions.

These publicly funded programs operate locally in cities throughout the country, often with additional private financial support, and offer young people ages fourteen to twenty-four summer work experience for a set number of weeks. Youth employment programs are designed specifically to enhance the employability of young people by supporting them with opportunities and helping them work through barriers to employment.

Along with the specific work opportunity, these programs typically offer training and workshops on topics like workplace etiquette basics and money management. Some programs may offer guidance on entrepreneurship and others may include resume help, interviewing tips, and career counseling so that young people can identify their interests.

The Abdul Latif Jameel Poverty Action Lab (J-PAL), a global research center focused on reducing poverty, summarized thirteen academic papers evaluating summer job programs in Boston, Chicago, New York, and Philadelphia and found numerous benefits of youth employment programs such as increasing the earnings of young people living in a low-income household and reducing involvement in the criminal justice system.[11]

In a separate study that followed summer employment participants in Ohio, evidence found that youth were less likely to have both delinquency filings and to be incarcerated in the adult jail system two years after placement than were individuals in the matched comparison group. Participants also had better school attendance rates in the academic year following summer employment and were more likely to graduate from high school compared to other youth.[12] There are numerous benefits to these kinds of government- and nonprofit-sponsored summer jobs programs that merit even greater investment from decision-makers.

3. Social Enterprises

Because executive functioning is still developing for young people, early work experiences create an opportunity to expose adolescents and young adults to these skills and integrate them into workforce development programs.

Employment social enterprises are a growing business model that allows for the goals of profit and customer service to blend with the need for talent and the need for young people to gain pathways into employment.

Profit is not the primary goal of these businesses. They sell high-quality goods and services, then invest the money they make into their business and the people who work in it—paying a livable wage and providing employees services that affect their ability to work, like access to childcare, job coaching, and mental health services.

The Chicago-based nonprofit New Moms is creating employment opportunities for new mothers through a social enterprise model. It believes in the strength, skills, and resiliency of young mothers ages twenty-four and younger. It has a comprehensive program that helps with housing; provides paid job training, coaching, and transportation support for parents in college; and gives overall family support to help the care of mother and child.

To support employment, New Moms runs a sixteen-week job training program at its candle-making company and designs it to be a positive learning environment with real-life work experience to practice skills. Participants are paired with a coach and placed in small groups, go through a curriculum that includes classroom-based strengths assessments, set goals for their career and education, and participate in workshops on interviewing and resumes. The participants get hands-on practice at the candle-making company Bright Endeavors, and the program ends with job placement support.

The entire program was developed with a brain-based approach and focus on executive skills so that the moms enrolled can learn while they get support with organizing, planning, and completing work.

As with all things regarding young people, there is a role for parents and other caring adults to play in terms of helping and supporting youth prepare for work and choose the work opportunities that would best suit them. Youth who do not have these kinds of caring and connected relationships with adults or who are involved with the juvenile justice or foster care systems require tremendous employment support. Creative solutions are needed to get all young people early work experiences.

Data show why young people and specific groups of adolescents need more support. In 2022, the overall U.S. unemployment rate was 3.6 percent. That same year, the unemployment rate for people ages sixteen to twenty-four was 9.4 percent.[13]

When broken out by race, it's clear that some young people need more employment support. In 2023, the unemployment rate was 7 percent for white youth, 10.5 percent for Hispanic youth, and 18 percent for Black youth.

There is also another category of young people ages sixteen to twenty-four who are not in the workforce or in school. They are often referred to as disconnected, vulnerable, or opportunity youth. Data show that the youth populations struggling the most with connecting to school or work opportunities have less education, come from low-income families, and belong to a racial or ethnic minority.[14]

What young people with barriers to early work opportunities need is a different approach to those initial work experiences. Casey's Generation Work program, an initiative across five cities, looks at both the needs of employers and the support youth workers need to succeed. Through mentoring and work-based learning, young people can prepare themselves for work.

In the Generation Work approach, employers are carefully cultivated to participate in the program, with their employment needs and work culture deeply understood and taken into account. Meanwhile, for the youth participants, the program takes a positive youth development approach. (I will talk more about youth development in Chapter 8, but it involves focusing on a young person's strengths, assets, and competencies to prepare them for success in adulthood.)

In the Indianapolis site, young people needed literacy coaching so that they could earn a degree and be set up for work opportunities. In Philadelphia, young people received career coaching that helped them earn certifications and credentials for health care and human services jobs.

Overall, the approach is to provide opportunities that recognize the full experience of what a young person has gone through, including experience with the justice system and trauma, as well as the responsibilities they may have, such as caring for families and children. Through experiences such as volunteerism, job training, and service learning, youth and young adults learn how to use their skills and talents to make a positive contribution and build relationships with caring adults. Those experiences can then be a model for future work experiences.

Financial Management and Literacy

When adjusted for inflation, wages have remained virtually the same since 1980, but those numbers represent the overall average.[15] As a result, many young workers, who are often trapped in lower-wage jobs due to their lower skills, are just getting by. About 53 million Americans as young as eighteen and up to age sixty-four qualify as low-wage workers—about 44 percent of the workforce.

Their median hourly wages are $10.22 and median annual earnings are about $18,000.[16] About 13 percent of those people are youth ages eighteen to twenty-four. The median hourly wage for them is $8.55 and the median annual salary is $12,672.[17]

That means that average earnings for a working young adult do not provide enough income for them to support themselves. Furthermore, many low-income young adults and young adults of color must contribute to their family's household finances. This affects their ability to save long term.

Either way, as young people earn wages, they must acquire the skill of financial literacy. Just like a young person's entry into the workplace, building one's financial capability is not an automatic process. Young people need reputable guidance and support to learn how to do this instead of relying on the unverified advice they may find on the internet or through social media. Without it, they may struggle with money management for their entire lives—it is a skill that many adults still struggle with.

Although financial literacy is a challenge for many adults, for adolescents it is especially difficult. That's because their developing brains are wired for taking risks and primed to seek rewards. That makes the idea of spending money an attractive, exciting option compared to saving, budgeting, or investing. So, as their executive functioning continues to strengthen, it makes sense to impart money management lessons. Practicing money management skills allows young people to learn how to make choices that allow them to enjoy life today while also creating security in their financial future.

For example, the United Way of Delaware believes people at every income level and in every neighborhood deserve financial stability, including adolescents. It created a free financial coaching program, Stand By Me, so state residents can reach their money goals and have peace of mind.

The program for adolescents, Stand By Me NexGen, is aimed

at high school students. It goes beyond the basics of how money works and connects money management to work and education opportunities after high school. The goal of its "College, Careers, & Cash" program is to help adolescents understand the connection between making good career and financial decisions and being an independent adult consumer who can successfully make those decisions. They use workshops and interactive experiences to help young people better understand their money, identify their financial goals, and begin to make wise financial decisions and be on the road to financial stability.

With a foundation of financial literacy and coaching, young people can better evaluate their financial options. As adolescents continue to grow, mature, and start to work, these kinds of coaching programs are an example of the tangible support they can receive.

The lessons teach young people to understand how money works, including identifying future financial goals like saving money, building credit, and growing assets. The tailored financial instruction also gives them a road map for the financial reality of college and their early career.

Financial literacy and coaching are important but are also just one part of the financial landscape young people must navigate. They will encounter financial decisions at every turn, from ads for crypto investments, to newer ways to make installment payments on purchases through tools like AfterPay, to endless credit card offers. I remember when I got my first bank account at age sixteen (I still use it, by the way, even though it has changed bank names at least five times) and later applied for my first credit card. These are critical financial and personal milestones that can either set up a young person for success for years to come or put them on a difficult financial path.

The catch is that many financial products offer young people an opportunity to spend more than they have. And smartphones give young people easy access to potentially predatory financial opportunities. Given their risk appetite, many young adults may find themselves in situations where they have acquired debt with a high interest rate, which affects their ability to budget and meet other financial obligations. This is why young people need programs and employers who teach them the basics of money management.

Work for young people is critically important. It helps them figure out what they enjoy doing and how to successfully manage the financial rewards of their effort. And if they are lucky, work also provides them with more than just skills and compensation. It can also be an outlet through which they learn how to constructively express their ideas and opinions.

Finding their voice and learning to advocate for themselves and others is an expression of the highest level on Maslow's hierarchy. Being able to express yourself in ways that influence others is a key skill leading to self-esteem and self-actualization. The next chapter will give more details on the role and importance of youth engagement and leadership and why it benefits us all.

8

Youth Leadership: Taking Charge of Their Lives

Naomi Wadler stepped to the microphone in front of a crowd of thousands as if she had done it many times before. At age eleven, she was making her public speaking debut at the 2022 March for Our Lives, a protest against gun violence.

Her journey to that moment began after a personal connection to gun violence. She knew the daughter of her mother's friend, who was a student at Parkland High School and died in the shooting that killed a total of fifteen adolescents and two teachers. Naomi watched as high schoolers protested after the shooting and staged walkouts. She found herself wanting to follow in their footsteps and represent others who might see something of themselves in her—a young, Black, Ethiopian, and Jewish girl.

"And I felt that, even though they were so much older than me, that I could do that too," she said. "Because I've never really seen someone who looked like me, or who was around the same age as me, or shared those common things with me." [1]

She took to the stage and announced that she was there to represent Black girls and women on the issue of gun control and to give them a voice. Now seventeen, Naomi has spent her teen years continuing her advocacy—giving media interviews and speaking around the world about making a difference and addressing societal problems and injustice. She has also been busy being a typical adolescent, debating with her mother about her access to social media and celebrating her bat mitzvah.[2]

There are thousands of young people like Naomi right now making a difference in their communities and advocating on behalf of young people and on issues that matter most to them. There are many more in the making. Their passion, emotion, hard work, and empathy for others are visible and vibrant. As young people grow and mature, we want more of them to use their voices similarly on behalf of others.

But first, they have to find their voice.

The developing brain during adolescence is more active in the amygdala area, which is responsible for feelings, desires, and emotions. Anyone who has spent time with some adolescents can see and feel their sense of passion and determination not to accept things as they are, but to believe and want to make an earnest effort to change things for the better. That desire for change starts with young people expressing their thoughts or feelings about themselves and their life. From there it can grow to weighing in on a topic or situation—similar to Naomi Wadler deciding that she wasn't going to let her youth be a barrier to speaking out on gun violence. All through adolescence, young people are expanding their ability to determine their perspective and advocate for themselves. They are learning to express their needs, assert their rights, and actively participate in decisions that affect their lives.

This kind of personal agency looks different at age thirteen when compared to age eighteen or age twenty-three because it is a gradual learning process tied to the deliberate maturity of the adolescent brain. Teen brains shift from relying on emotion and desires in the more active amygdala area to understanding self-control and consequences when the brain's prefrontal cortex is fully developed.

During adolescence, young people also develop the necessary skills, confidence, and understanding to navigate the many different complexities of their lives. As this happens, they can better appreciate the outcomes of various actions. They also grow their ability to craft thoughtful arguments and to listen to others with empathy that makes their position more influential.

Initially, young people find their voice on issues related to themselves. They are getting to know their interests and desires better, and they are taking critical steps toward designing a life that is uniquely theirs. This is the foundation of self-advocacy.

When young people deploy these skills on behalf of others and their community, they are practicing youth leadership. To be truly independent human beings and contributing members of society, all young people can actively direct their lives and shape the communities they live in. Both concepts are examples of youth engagement, which I will explore in this chapter.

According to Jennifer Tackett, a clinical psychologist at Northwestern University, adolescence is a window of opportunity for creating a new generation of changemakers because of several physiological and emotional factors. "The rapid development of personality, peer relationships, values and vocational identity during this period, make adolescence an optimal time for developing leadership potential," Tackett wrote in a journal article about leadership and adolescents.[3]

An adolescent developing the ability to advocate for themselves is significant. It empowers them by giving them a sense of control over their minds and bodies. They start to realize that they are growing into a unique and distinct individual and that realization fuels their desire and growing confidence to make decisions about their lives.

An adolescent's ability to express themselves and assert their personal needs is a positive contributing factor to a young person's overall mental health. It can help to reduce feelings of helplessness and foster a sense of control over one's circumstances. With a brain more sensitive to emotions during this developmental period, young people need to communicate their wishes and desires so they can get adult support in addressing how they feel, especially if things feel overwhelming.

During adolescence, the brain is active in the areas that are peer-focused—meaning relationships with friends take on a heightened focus. Within that experience, self-advocacy becomes even more critical for young people so that they can navigate with increasing confidence the social and peer relationships that grow in importance during these years. Self-advocacy in this way looks like setting boundaries in these relationships so youth can try to stay true to their values in the face of peer pressure.

Adults play a critical role in providing the space and support for emerging adults to practice and perfect all these engagement and advocacy skills. That's because adults can model the behavior they want adolescents to emulate. Doing this creates partnership between both parties, each with specific roles to play. Adults need to accept and encourage adolescents to have a say about what is happening in their lives and to consider their perspective. Adolescents need to be open to taking time to learn communication—analytical and decision-making skills that will increase the chances that they are heard and understood.

This kind of partnership is not something that all adults or organizations typically seek out or embrace. Many adults may not see the need to prepare young people to advocate for themselves in this way. Too often adults have negative stereotypes about young people—things like they are not wise enough or too immature to handle making life decisions. We often get frustrated at a young person's early attempts to have us consider their opinions.

We often don't view young people as experts in themselves. We think as adults that we have all the solutions and know what's best based on research, data, and our own experience—and have no need to hear from young people. But as they mature into adulthood, adolescents need to be recognized as individuals who have the most critical perspective on what is happening in their lives.

They also have key insights about the challenges they face and often creative ideas that would improve how they approach and choose solutions.

I have been through the experience of thinking I had the answer as an adult but learning a new approach from an adolescent—in this case, my daughter.

I vividly recall trying to help her navigate a difficult relationship with her eighth-grade science teacher. He didn't seem to see the best in her and constantly criticized her behavior in class. I know that she is highly social and was probably chatting with friends in ways that may have been disruptive, but his reactions seemed out of proportion to the offense. If she said nothing, he complained that she wasn't participating. If she spoke out, he wrote her up for talking too much. After surviving his class, she went on to ninth grade and I hoped she wouldn't have to engage with this teacher ever again.

But it turned out he was the advisor for the eighth-grade trip, which featured ninth graders who could apply to be peer leaders. This was a leadership opportunity that Lauren wanted. I advised her not to apply, fearing this teacher would either not select her or would find a problem with her if he did. But she told me it was an important growth opportunity for her and she wanted to apply, just to show this teacher who she was. I was supportive but skeptical.

Surprisingly, she was selected. And even more amazingly, the teacher wrote to tell me how positively and professionally Lauren showed up and how impressed he was with her. It turned out her personality was a real asset on the trip, helping more reluctant students engage. She is a natural and decisive leader with charisma that many young people and adults are drawn to. I couldn't have been prouder of her. She took the initiative to demonstrate who she was as a person and gained so much confidence in her ability to speak up for herself, make decisions that are right for her, and be the person she wanted to be. Her cautious mama was wrong.

I have noted before how the dynamic development of the adolescent brain mirrors the brain growth that humans make from birth to age three. During that time, for example, babies learn to walk—and once they get the hang of it, they go off in different directions and situations. We guide them to make sure they don't cross into the street or walk into other danger. But we don't want to restrict their movement; it is a toddler's necessary exploration in their discovery of the world.

It is similar for adolescents, who are learning which new and different directions they want to go in as they grow up and seek their place in the world. It is also similar for parents in that we want to guide our teenagers through their journey and protect them from potential danger. But we also know deep down that we can't restrict them from exploring and trying things on their own because that is part of growing up.

There are benefits to youth and adults building this kind of respectful and cooperative partnership. It allows adults to let go of the pressure of being the sole make-or-break force in a young person's life. By contrast, it allows young people to practice the problem-solving skills they will need in adulthood and gives them opportunities to strengthen the parts of the brain that drive those skills.[4] Adults and youth coming together collaboratively helps young people build their self-esteem and leadership skills. That can have the effect of increasing a young person's influence among their peers and in their community.

At the Casey Foundation, we have seen three core values that help develop successful partnerships between young people and adults and support youth engagement.

First, young people must be effectively prepared and empowered to make informed decisions about matters that affect their lives. That means adults put in the time and effort to work with young people and build relationships with them so young people are receptive to the lessons to be imparted. To do this, adults need to believe that young people have natural strengths and positive attributes that need to be cultivated and developed. It's about balancing power dynamics between young people and adults and believing that all kids are everyone's kids.

One of the benefits of adults preparing young people to take charge of their lives is that adolescents get to practice firsthand when and how to seek advice and counsel from professionals and other caring adults. This is an essential life skill, especially at a time when the development of the adolescent brain prioritizes peer relationships. The benefit of adults working to prepare young people in this way is that it strengthens the youth-adult relationship and helps to foster a bond of trust that gives young people the foundation to design their lives. It also creates a safe space for young people to address their knowledge gaps—a kind of trial-and-error no judgment zone as they acquire new communication and personal development skills. The entire process allows young people to grow and assert their leadership as they learn to make decisions on their own behalf.

The second core value is that young people have a network of supportive relationships that gives them customized and tailored support. This can take many forms.

In Chapter 6 I talked about the importance of transformative relationships—trusted bonds between youth and adults that significantly shape a young person's life. These are visible in everything from the informal guidance from elders at family gatherings to formal resources through a nonprofit training program. In these instances, a youth's relationship with adults is the vehicle to transmit the support to a young person so that they can acknowledge it, receive it, and use it as a foundation for their growth.

Young people in the juvenile justice or child welfare system are supposed to be provided formal support such as mentoring, classes, training, coaching, counseling, and much more. Human service systems have a responsibility to provide young people with programs and access to services that are relevant to their lived experiences and personal and cultural background, and that are attentive to their overall well-being. As a result, it is critical for public systems to listen to the consumers they serve as they design and run their programs.

Finally, adolescents need opportunities for self-development. It is through these kinds of opportunities that they get new ideas and inspiration for which direction they want their lives to go. These opportunities include healthy risk-taking, such as being exposed to new experiences and activities so that they can learn what they like or don't like, to help positively shape their identity.

It's not always easy for adults to let young people make more decisions, build a network of advisors beyond them, and give them more independence through opportunities for self-development. Our ideas about how young people should grow and develop get in the way. But adolescent brain science supports youth being able to count on adults for the preparation, support, and opportunity to advocate for themselves.

At Casey, we have an ongoing youth-adult partnership in our Jim Casey Initiative, a way for young people who have experience with the foster care system to draw on their experiences, perspectives, ideas, and skills to advance reforms in the system.[5]

The young people selected for the program work directly with adults in a way where they are treated as equal partners. They codesign and facilitate training for child welfare professionals and they are invited to speak or participate in high-profile meetings.

The difference between these opportunities and simply highlighting the story of a young person is that all of the activities are done with the idea that the experience must grow the skills and develop the young person, not just benefit the adult from learning about the youth's firsthand perspective. An example of what this looks like in practice is if there is an ongoing working group, the young person would receive the agenda and background materials in advance just like the other group members so that they would be prepared to meaningfully participate in the meeting.

Youth learning how to advocate on their own behalf through leadership experiences is a critically important skill on the road to adulthood. It takes on an even bigger importance based on the circumstances in which they are growing up. For youth who are in the child welfare and juvenile justice system, being able to advocate for themselves has very high stakes.

"Who do you want to live with?"

"What do you want to do after you are released?"

"What kind of support do you need to fulfill your personal goals?"

Typically, adults in positions of authority are posing these kinds of questions to youth who have experienced multiple traumas. Those traumatic experiences make it less likely that a young person feels confident or comfortable to express what it is that they want to happen to them. They might not even feel like they have the power to articulate such a thing, even when invited to give their perspective.

Plus, young people in these circumstances are often living with people who are not family. As a result, they have to learn how to advocate without supportive adults around them, or perhaps without ever having an adult model that kind of behavior to them. This is a tall order, especially when their ability or inability to articulate what they need has far-reaching implications for their present living situation and the rest of their lives.

There is a growing movement in juvenile justice to empower the youth in the system to share their experiences as a way to advocate for much-needed changes that would affect them and others. In New Mexico, a youth group of sixteen- to nineteen-year-olds called Leaders Organizing 2 Unite and Decriminalize (LOUD) was created with officials from the local government (Bernalillo County Juvenile Detention Alternatives Initiative) and a nonprofit (New Mexico Forum for Youth in Community).[6] The goal was to bring youth together and empower them to give voice to their experiences to help create positive change in the juvenile justice system.

Many members of LOUD were formerly incarcerated youth. They worked alongside adults to research the over-criminalization of young people of color. Their method was to create a survey to look at the experiences young people had with the system: court hearings, detention, long-term facilities, residential treatment programs, specialty programs, and mental health services.

Members of LOUD also conducted four focus groups inside a state youth detention center, and four additional focus groups in specialty court programs, such as drug court. They also served as an informal youth council for the local justice system and gave input on its policies and practices. Based on all of this work, the group provided recommendations to improve county juvenile justice services in New Mexico and presented their findings to county officials. The results were that the group offered a new vision for juvenile justice based on lived experience in the system.[7]

This is just one example of the powerful ways that young people, especially young people in challenging circumstances, can work with adults to find their voice. They are still adolescents and these are formative experiences that are crucial to their personal growth and brain development. It is also a powerful reminder that young people can advocate on behalf of their peers by sharing the experience of what it is like being an adolescent and coming of age.

Adolescent leaders I have talked about in previous chapters, like Sixto Cancel and Nicole Lynn Lewis, are examples of taking on advocacy leadership roles with their lived experiences and creating solutions that help others. When young people develop this kind of self-agency, they can lead themselves and make meaningful change for others.

History has shown that they also can lead movements. From the Civil Rights Movement to the Arab Spring to school shooting survivors and advocates, there is a special mix of optimism and energy that young people have to create change—and this shows up in adolescence. This is a powerful period to develop the next generation of leaders.

Young people have long been leading organized movements for fairness and freedom. Gwen Sanders Gamble was only sixteen years old when she organized and trained other young people in Alabama to march in the Birmingham Children's Crusade to protest segregation. While still in high school, Moctesuma Esparza, along with other Chicano students, organized the East L.A. Walkouts, which demanded educational equity for Chicano students in California. At fifteen, Greta Thunberg sat outside the Swedish parliament by herself in protest against climate change, inspiring similar protests around the world and sparking a youth climate change movement. In Pakistan, Malala Yousafzai started an anonymous blog at age eleven to detail life under Taliban rule. Years later, she was shot in the head on her way home from school, yet survived the attack, becoming a global advocate for girls being allowed to attend school.

Youth who are prepared, supported, and allowed to weigh in on what is best for their lives can take the journey to adulthood with growing confidence that they are responsible for their lives. Some may grow eager to take on responsibilities for their communities and the most pressing issues of the day.

Adults have a vital role to play in this process; they can encourage and guide young people as needed but also give adolescents the space and breathing room they need to make their decisions and learn from them. Adults should view the young person's feelings and decisions as valid and give them weight, respecting them and not patronizing them.

Young people need more autonomy on the road to adulthood, but they won't be able to navigate the journey alone. It will take the participation, cooperation, and coordination of the public and private systems that touch the lives of millions of American youth.

Just as adults who work directly with young people need to shed misconceptions about young people and play a new kind of role in their development, so do the business leaders, nonprofit executives, and officials from public institutions. The leadership of these critical sectors needs to understand and take an active role in helping adolescents thrive into adulthood.

In Part III, I will discuss the role and responsibility for each of these five critical sectors of society that shape the lives of young people: nonprofits and philanthropy, business, public systems and policymakers, families, and communities.

PART III

A Call to Action to Thrive

9

The Ecosystem It Takes to Thrive

My daughter Lauren had an opportunity when she was nine years old that many young people never get—to leave her neighborhood and travel internationally to Costa Rica with her Girl Scout troop. I had the resources and the job flexibility to go with her.

The trip goal was for the troop to learn about and experience the Central American country's unique landscape, plants, and animals. On the trip, the girls enjoyed exploring the jungle with its giant trees and leaves bigger than their heads. The girls saw wildly colorful poison dart frogs, turtles, butterflies, snakes, iguanas, and the occasional sloth. The diverse landscape also included volcanoes, beaches, and rainforests.

Costa Rica is a bit smaller than West Virginia, yet it has about 6 percent of the world's biodiversity. To make sure the country remains viable for future generations, 25 percent of Costa Rica is protected by the administrative Sistema Nacional de Áreas de Conservación (National System of Conservation Areas).[1] We were fortunate that this protection enabled us to enjoy the natural beauty of Costa Rica's unique environment.

It was just the kind of eye-opening and life-changing experience that too many of their third-grade peers lack access to. In this place so different from their homes in Baltimore, the girls learned that Costa Rica's rich mix of plants and animals exists in a delicate balance known as an ecosystem.

In biological terms, an ecosystem consists of every organism present in a specific environment or place.[2] Ecosystems are complex and the interactions between the diverse elements make them interdependent. The very biodiversity that is the hallmark of an ecosystem contributes to its stability. This is because the wide array of plants and animals learn to adapt to changing conditions, and therefore are more likely to survive disturbances, disease, and climate change.

Humans, too, need biodiversity to survive. As I consider what it takes for adolescents to thrive, I realize that these same principles are as true for their development as they are for their physical survival. To nurture their well-being, along with the material and emotional support I have talked about in previous chapters, young people need healthy and protected environments to grow.

Children and youth are profoundly shaped and affected by the people, conditions, resources, and influences around them. It is within this context that they access the relationships, resources, and opportunities required to mature into healthy and happy adults.

In the first two sections of this book, I shared background on the adolescent brain, how it develops, and five key areas of a young person's life that are shaped by their developing brains. All of that information focuses on the young person and their experiences as they grow and mature.

This last section explores *where and how* adolescents grow up. These environments determine whether they will have access to people beyond family members who will support and encourage them, enriching experiences that prepare them for educational and employment success, and resources to meet their basic needs. All of these ingredients—if amply and appropriately provided—will positively shape the trajectory of their lives into healthy adults.

In this chapter, I describe the adolescent ecosystem: its

environmental factors and the entities within these structures that have a deep influence on the ability of adolescents to thrive into adulthood.

Urie Bronfenbrenner was an influential child psychologist who developed a framework called the Ecological Systems Theory to explain the influence of a child's environment on their development. Before Bronfenbrenner, researchers used to study childhood separately from other people and factors. Child psychologists studied children while anthropologists studied society, sociologists studied families, economists studied the economy, and political scientists studied the structures of society.[3]

However, Bronfenbrenner focused his work on understanding how children are affected by the context in which they grow up—especially children in poverty. He defined layers of environment expanding outward from those closest to a child (such as family and community environments), to layers that are further away from their immediate lives (like larger societal contexts). Each affects a child's development.[4] Bronfenbrenner believed that real-life environments where children lived and grew had a profound impact on their development. He emphasized in his work the need to go beyond a child's personality, individual experiences, or reaction to controlled stimuli and seek to understand the interplay and interaction of the child's relationships with the people and organizations around them.

His theory influenced how people understood the need to surround children and their families with a strong support system to increase the likelihood of their success. Based on this knowledge, he helped to establish the federal Head Start program, which provides comprehensive education, health, nutrition, and parent involvement services to young children in low-income families.[5]

At the heart of Bronfenbrenner's Ecological Systems Theory is the idea that children do not develop in isolation. They grow up and become themselves within the context of their relationships and interactions with their surroundings, both the physical conditions in which they live and the people and processes that affect them.[6]

Applying the concept of an ecosystem to our understanding of adolescents requires considering the invisible web of people, networks, and interactions that govern their daily lives, and appreciating whether that ecosystem functions in an integrated and predictable way to influence young people's life outcomes. When the connections within the youth ecosystem are healthy and geared to an adolescent's well-being, the ecosystem helps young people grow and thrive in adulthood. Fractures and gaps in the youth ecosystem, on the other hand, can leave young people stuck on the bridge to adulthood, unable to move forward.

Elements of the Adolescent Ecosystem

While we know from brain science that peers are influential in the lives of adolescents, families sit at the heart of the youth ecosystem. They play the most important role and have the greatest potential to serve as a protective force. Families ideally are closest to the young person and are typically the people who have the longest history with them and know them the best. Research shows that children need families to thrive and are most likely to succeed as adults when at least one parent or other caring adult has a lifelong, stable, and committed relationship with them.[7] As such, parents and families have a crucial role in helping make sure that the young people in their lives are on the right track and get what they need from and through the variety of entities around them.

Parents play a tremendous role in preparing adolescents for adulthood in innumerable ways. They encourage school success and partner with teachers to address areas of academic weakness. They teach resilience in the face of failure. They support a child's career dreams and the exploration and preparation to make those dreams a reality. Most important, they make sure a child's basic needs are met, and that they know they are loved and belong. A strong family foundation produces a consistency to an adolescent's journey, a sense of acceptance, and an unverbalized feeling of assurance that they are going to "make it." A young person with a strong family knows that as they cross the bridge between childhood and adulthood at least one person has their back along the way.[8]

Beyond their immediate family, ideally young people should have neighbors, family friends, peers, and community members who are also invested in their success. This kind of support system provides both a protective factor and an accelerant to success.

The African proverb, "It takes a village to raise a child," is often mentioned in discussions around child-rearing. It refers to the concept that children need many people (the village) to provide a safe, healthy environment to experience the physical and emotional security they need to be able to realize their life's hopes and dreams. Inherent in the necessity of this village is the notion that helping children develop is a responsibility we all share, not just parents.

The youth ecosystem also includes government: federal, state, and local agencies that manage services for the benefit of the public. Some government services, such as public health programs and parks and recreation centers, are designed to serve everyone, regardless of age. Other systems, such as K–12 public schools, pediatric and adolescent health care, the child welfare system, and the juvenile justice system, on the other hand, specifically serve children and youth.

The effectiveness of government agencies depends on many factors, including how well policies are crafted and implemented—processes that can go unseen unless you are directly affected.

For others, however, especially low-income youth and their families who depend on their ecosystem to meet a wider array of basic needs, you could imagine how any systemic gap or failure in government poses a real threat to their immediate and long-term well-being. You can also imagine that a system that separates children from their families—such as child welfare or juvenile justice—could cause real harm if those kinds of decisions are not designed with the important connections to caring adults, education, and opportunity at their core.

When adolescents seek their employment, private employers become part of the youth ecosystem. Employers offer training opportunities for young people and provide early work experiences that can help them get a financial foothold into adulthood.

Nonprofits represent another powerful piece of the adolescent ecosystem. They complement the roles of government and employers in society and can contribute to a young person's quality of life. Nonprofits help families and youth meet their basic needs through entities like food banks and hospitals. Institutions like museums also contribute to cultural and artistic expression. After-school programs can complement educational institutions and keep young people safe and engaged.

These varied organizations I have described would ideally create a complex and interdependent network of private, nonprofit, and public entities that young people can trust and depend on. It would operate in reliable and predictable ways to support their daily activities and growth. When you combine this network with the physical, political, and economic features of society, the invisible ecosystem in which each young person lives becomes clear. This ecosystem affects nearly every aspect of a young person's daily experience, for good or ill.

Yet too many young people don't have the positive inputs in this ecosystem around them to set them up for success. We've seen these kinds of "system failures" in Baltimore where young people have said they are eager for employment, recreation, and other positive activities but felt like city and civic leaders weren't doing enough to create those kinds of opportunities.[9] Without systemic investments in programs and communities, loops of violence and trauma because of the prevailing infrastructure create barriers for young people at every turn. That leaves young people feeling like they are set up to fail and not succeed.

We—and by *we* I mean all of us—must envision and see ourselves and our organizations as essential elements of an adolescent's life. While parents and caregivers, peers, and community have large roles to play, no one person, institution, organization, or parent alone can provide what young people need to thrive. Rather, it takes the entirety of an engaged and coordinated ecosystem of services and support for young people to thrive into adulthood.

Strengthening the Ecosystem

It would be great to imagine that the various entities that a young person encounters are all performing their roles in a finely choreographed dance designed to ensure adolescents cross the bridge to adulthood successfully. In reality, the situation is completely different. In any of these interactions, young people are navigating distinct and separate, complex sets of people and processes often focused only on one aspect of their lives.

When you consider the power that this ecosystem holds over a child's life, we should all be deeply concerned about any gaps, rejection, inconsistencies, and lack of coordination. As young people cross the bridge to adulthood, these deficits in their ecosystem are akin to rough winds, missing steps, and going forward without a guide—greatly decreasing the likelihood that they will successfully make the crossing. Some adolescents are more affected by these gaps than others, especially adolescents growing up in low-income households, youth of color and immigrant families, or those who are in foster care or the juvenile justice system.

Costa Rica has a formal authority to protect the wildlife in their country's physical ecosystem. For humans, how do we protect and nurture adolescents when there is no formal authority for them?

Building Healthy and Healing Relationships with Adults and Peers (Rejection and Belonging)

Relationships, including those with family and friends, are critically important in a youth ecosystem. It is through relationships that young people either experience a sense of rejection or belonging and feel as if they can be their true selves within a setting or community.[10] A sense of belonging promotes feelings of security, value, affirmation, connection, and alignment with others. As they navigate physical, emotional, and psychological changes, adolescents want to explore their identity and express themselves knowing that they are in environments that will accept them. During this vulnerable period in their lives when they are learning to take the lead, young people need to feel safe while they explore and experiment.

What does that look like for adolescents? The Forum for Youth Investment, a leading nonprofit organization that works on developing youth and strengthening the ecosystem around them, surveyed young people around the country to find out what they think. This is what the young people said:

- A caring relationship is "one person that we can connect with and feel like we belong to, that way people would not feel so left out in the world."
- A supportive environment provides "access to spaces where we can learn new things and be inspired by each other."
- Acceptance means "having people listen to us more, rather than respond, dictate, or debate."[11]

What these young people are describing is a sense of belonging. In recent years, the Forum has taken a comprehensive look at the critical issue of belonging as it relates to the environment around young people. It is deeply connected to the science of the developing adolescent brain discussed in previous chapters.

The adolescent brain undergoes developmental changes that refine circuits linked to empathy, sensitivity to social cues, and emotional understanding. It would make sense then that young people are looking for environments where they feel accepted and connected, rather than judged. They are looking to cultivate social-emotional skills by reflecting what their surroundings provide.

Adolescence is also a time when young people are forming their identity. As a result, the kinds of environments where they might feel a sense of belonging could change with that shifting sense of self. For the young people who also are navigating foster care or involvement in the juvenile justice system, it is even more important that the relationships in their ecosystem focus on building their strengths rather than defining them and their potential by the mistakes they or their parents have made.

We must ensure the entire ecosystem around all adolescents is attuned to their inherent need to experience nurturing, supportive, and affirming relationships. And we must do this not just for young people, but to ensure a brighter future, stronger communities, and economic prosperity for all of us. As Frederick Douglass famously said: "It is easier to build strong children than to repair broken men."

Navigation
When I had to cross the scary Arouca 516 bridge, I didn't do it alone. I had a guide who could tell me what to do to stay safe, how best to get across, and what I could expect on the journey. That's what young people need as they navigate adolescence.

But they need more than just one person, because this is an intricate and extended journey. Without a series of guides helping them not only navigate and understand the implications of each step but get to the next one, many young people end up independently learning how to discern and take advantage of opportunities. Those who are lucky find their way through these systems via a process of trial and error, luck, and adult helpers—sometimes personal, other times provided by public and private entities. This issue of how to navigate the ecosystem is something that all adolescents must confront.

When we think of the word navigation, we might first think about a cell phone with a map app telling us how to get from point A to B (or point C) in the physical world. Navigation for adolescents isn't usually this straightforward, but in many ways, it should be. In this context, navigation describes the help young people need as they move through a process or system—say, applying for a job—especially when their skills or life experiences haven't prepared them to be successful.[12] It's also helpful guidance for adolescents to look beyond those immediate steps and think about the future implications of the choices they're making now.

As noted previously, young people interact with all kinds of governmental, nonprofit, employment, and community organizations that rarely coordinate with one another. That leaves young people to figure out for themselves how to piece together everything they need and how to understand complex processes. For example, young people aspiring to attend college are sometimes largely on their own trying to determine which school is the best for them out of hundreds of options. Then they must make it through the specific application instructions—asking for and receiving teacher recommendations, writing essays at the appropriate word count, and uploading all of the information electronically as requested. Then, if a young person is accepted, they must complete paperwork by certain deadlines and also figure out how to get their studies paid for—which triggers a whole separate application process.

At the same time, young people are trying to figure out their place in the world. They are trying to connect their educational experiences to what they may want to do next, whether that's further education or starting a career. They also are navigating the many different relationships in their lives: with each other, their parents and families, and the larger community.

Consider the significant navigation tasks we place on young people to be successful in their late teens when we know that the part of their brains (the prefrontal cortex) that is used for executive functioning, complex analysis, and decision-making isn't fully mature until age twenty-five! We are asking them to take on tasks they aren't equipped to complete independently but can learn with the help of caring adults.

Parents can be a main source of support for their children as they are navigating all of these different aspects of adolescence, whether those are personal experiences or experiences with systems. But this relationship serves a purpose beyond affirmation. Parents and caregivers play an essential role in helping young people navigate their ecosystem to obtain the resources and experiences they will need as they mature. Young people are trying to find their way through a web of dynamic situations within and across agencies, private employers, and nonprofits—intricate and interdependent just like the Costa Rican jungle.

Gaps and Inconsistencies

A healthy youth ecosystem would seamlessly connect networks, guidance, and support for young people from one step to the next. But we know there are gaps in the youth ecosystem and that millions of young people fall through for reasons we adults could foresee and prevent. We know young people lack executive functioning skills, yet society constantly puts the onus on them to figure out how to assemble what they need from a disorganized ecosystem.

Those expectations, out of step with developmental science, put young people at risk of making decisions now that could affect them for years to come. Too often systems are set up to respond only after the worst consequences of a young person's decisions and actions have happened. After they have missed the chance to apply for an apprenticeship. Ruined their credit. Become unhoused. Gotten in trouble with the law. After their families are in full-blown crisis . . . instead of when those families needed just a bit of extra support.

During my years of working in the social sector, I have witnessed this tragic pattern on a broad scale. But what if all the adults, leaders, and institutions within the youth development ecosystem provided support and services to youth and families *before* a point of crisis? What if that support was designed to work *with* a young person's strengths and positive qualities, and their parents' aspirations for their child?

Wealthier families typically have the resources and know-how to address deficiencies in the ecosystem of their adolescent: private tutors for education gaps, personal coaches for sports advantages, and access to adults in their family or network who have attended prestigious universities or work at private businesses that can help ensure a smooth path to college and internships. Arguably half of young people do not have these advantages, making their attempts to navigate the bridge of adolescence perilous. In future chapters, I'll talk about what a stronger, more supportive and strengths-based ecosystem would look like for them, and for the government and social sector.

Getting Stuck: The Unhealthy Ecosystem

The reality is that many challenges prevent young people from being born into and growing up in supportive, healthy environments, leading to the barriers I described in detail in Chapter 2.

The Ecosystem It Takes to Thrive

As I think about the complexities young people face—some more than others—I am reminded of an afternoon I spent in the woods behind my Atlanta elementary school when I was six.

My first-grade teacher sent our class outside to look for spiderwebs, a challenging task because they were invisible except in the right light. But I remember realizing that they were everywhere. They would cling to our clothes and skin if we stepped in the wrong place. And we couldn't clear a web away without great effort.

That's how I think about the ecosystems that some children and families are a part of and navigate today. The complex webs all around us may not be easy to spot at first, but once you look closely, you can see them everywhere—and they are easy to get trapped in. A spiderweb is not constructed to be solid, but to trap its prey within and between its sticky, thin silk fibers.

Decades later, I can see evidence all around us of the unhealthy environments that get so many young people eternally stuck and unable to fulfill their potential. They're invisible, except in the right light or until we try to see them. And they're impossible to clear away simply by pulling at a single strand. These spiderwebs are comprised of every facet of a young person's life, including the health, education, employment, justice, and financial systems they must rely on to survive. Instead of healthy connection and support, these ecosystems create loops and layers of disadvantage that derail promising young lives.

The adolescent ecosystem has its strengths and challenges when supporting young people into adulthood so they can thrive. We can build on the strengths and work to address the gaps, sticky spots, and inconsistencies to reimagine how to assist youth on their journey.

A Call to Action

Despite and maybe even because of the complexity of the ecosystem that young people grow up in, each of us can make a real difference in a young person's life as actors in the systems and agencies that affect young people.

My goal in this part of the book is to speak directly to those who have the power to create environments where young people thrive. We want to arm you with the know-how to build supportive spaces that help kids and their families grow and succeed.

For adolescents on the road to adulthood, three main groups of people and organizations have a large influence over their journey. Each one has a critical role to play in the lives of young people in this developmental period:

- The government sector: The public agencies, the public servants in leadership, policymakers, and the judiciary that make up this sector have a public mandate to steward and protect young people and their families. To be effective, they must anchor their perspective on an adolescent's developmental need for more freedom and exploration, which goes beyond their typical protective and reactive approach to younger children.
- The private sector: Employers can provide opportunities for young people to experience their first jobs and structured ways for adolescents and young adults to learn about the world of work. Employers also have an indirect role in young people's lives as the workplaces of their parents.
- The social sector: The social sector is the term I will use to describe nonprofits and philanthropy. Many of these entities deliver programming and services directly to adolescents. Because of the knowledge they gain through their proximity, they have a unique opportunity and responsibility to shift how they engage with young people to shape their future and to teach young people how to shape their destinies.

Finally, I want to give some examples of what good coordination looks like across sectors and what infrastructure needs to be built to help make that happen.

In the next chapter, I will discuss how the government can better serve young people in a more proactive and coordinated way.

10

Public Systems and Policymakers

Two boys named Wes Moore shared a name and few more things in common. They both grew up in low-income families in Baltimore and were exposed to crime and violence. They both lacked the guidance of their fathers and, as juveniles, were picked up by the police for delinquent behavior. They both had people around them who warned them they needed to change their ways.

By the time they became adolescents, some critical differences shaped their path to adulthood. One Wes Moore had an extended family that provided consistent support and paid for him to go to military school where he eventually imagined a brighter future for himself and graduated. The other Wes Moore stayed in his neighborhood and completed a Job Corps training program while accumulating a juvenile record from selling drugs and violent confrontations and living with a day-to-day mindset shaped by the pressures of poverty.

One Wes Moore is now the governor of Maryland. The other Wes Moore was convicted of murder and is in prison serving a life sentence without parole.[1]

Their journeys to adulthood show how the intersection of personal choices, access to support, and interaction with systems shapes life trajectories, as described so eloquently in the book *The Other Wes Moore*. In this chapter, I will explore how public systems impact the trajectory of young lives.

I use the term public systems to refer to the government—the large, complex agencies that play some of the biggest roles in supporting youth and their families. These agencies provide education, workforce development, health care, waste removal, parks and recreation, and public safety, as well as access to basic needs such as food, housing, or childcare assistance for low-income families. Across all levels of government, these agencies make decisions on behalf of youth that affect their lives for future decades based on the professionals who execute policy decisions and deploy billions of dollars toward these essential services. Despite being called "systems," they are in reality often a patchwork of local, state, and federal agencies that perform their work through government workers and contracts with nonprofit and for-profit organizations. No matter how it's constructed, the government plays a critical role in the ecosystem of all young people's lives.

Beyond these agencies, the government structures we've had in place for decades play another crucial role in the adolescent ecosystem. They provide the legislative and regulatory framework that governs the lives of young people and their families. These rules apply not just to government agencies but also to nonprofits, private companies, and the interactions between youth and other organizations. In this way, our government has significant power to ensure that public policies and agency practices reflect everything we know about adolescent development.

In many cases, the professionals in these systems have direct access to young people and can develop deep insights into who they are and what they might need. However, knowledge alone about adolescents is insufficient to guarantee good outcomes. The ingrained dynamics of these large, complex systems are bigger than any individual's intention or effort.

As large bureaucracies, these systems often operate in crisis with limited staff, funding pressure, and heightened public attention. These factors can lead to a narrow focus on their agency's specific mandate. Actors within these systems rarely have the opportunity to act more comprehensively to meet the needs of the young people (and families) they are serving or identify ways to help them realize their potential.

I worked at UPS, a company that is extremely efficient at delivering packages. While this is completely different work than the immensely important responsibility of helping young people grow, UPS's efficiency started with the architecture of a system designed to anticipate problems before they occurred. I believe there are lessons from the business world that could improve the way public systems function. The problems and challenges facing young people are much more complex, and the stakes far higher. All the more reason for us to build systems that best support dedicated professionals in the customized work of guiding each precious young person on their way.

Intervention vs. Prevention

UPS would never have survived as a company being reactionary. That would be like taking the most care and concern with customers only *after* losing their package.

Rather, the minute a package enters its care, UPS has developed an elaborate system to ensure on-time delivery and to prevent lost or damaged packages. It is not foolproof, but for a system that delivers 21 million packages a day around the world, less than 1 percent are lost or damaged in transit.

Surely the government must demand the same success rate for its role in stewarding human souls to adulthood and building a brighter future for all of its constituents. To do this well requires, as a start, anticipating the needs of each person; a skilled staff able to quickly solve problems and prioritize the ultimate goal; and tools like technology to track and measure success.

Many things in life and society operate from this kind of preventive approach. In dentistry, dentists put sealants on teeth to avoid cavities. We wear seatbelts and bike helmets to prevent injury in case of an accident. In sports, you have to play offense to win. But when it comes to working with children and youth, I have heard a litany of excuses about why we can't utilize a preventive approach even when it would produce better outcomes and cost less.

In child-serving public agencies, a lot of the work involves intervening *after* something has already happened to a young person or their family. Public dollars are in short supply and highly scrutinized. Many Americans believe in the ideal of rugged individualism—meaning people should focus on being self-reliant and independent from government assistance. As a result, proactive efforts to help families are often criticized as an inappropriate use of taxpayer dollars.

For example, nearly half of state and local child welfare funding supports placements of children in foster care or other out-of-home settings—while just 15 percent goes toward preventive services such as programs, training, and support that could strengthen families and keep children with their parents.[2] When you follow the money, it's clear that prevention is not a priority.

Reactive approaches are often a response to immediate and pressing needs, working under the misperception that the opportunity for prevention has passed, such as when families experience homelessness or a young person commits a crime. When this reactive approach is the case for not just a few families, but hundreds or thousands of them, many public systems become overwhelmed with the day-to-day demands of addressing crises and urgent situations. The staff in these public systems are unable to find the time or secure the buy-in from their leaders to prevent problems. Over time, choosing this firefighting approach over long-term prevention becomes the norm.

Consider the all-too-frequent case of a tragic situation like the death of a child who had been the subject of a child welfare investigation but was officially judged to be safe at home. This is certainly not the outcome we would want for any child, and systems must respond and take stock when it happens. But the reaction to such cases can have the unintended but real effect of causing further, less visible, but very real harm.

Instead of prompting analysis of how the system could have worked better before the tragedy or provided more support for this child to live in the best, safest environment possible from the start, the outcry from the public and media scrutiny often create political pressure to hastily fire agency leadership. That perpetuates the fear and overcorrection of more restrictive rules that deprive many other children of the conditions they need to grow up and thrive.

This, in turn, leads to an exaggerated fear of a child being seriously injured or dying while under the guardianship of state agencies, which leads to more children drawn into the system to avoid further criticism. A vicious cycle ensues that leaves even less capacity and resources to support families to stay together and prevent instability and unsafe environments. The results? In the name of accountability, new policies and procedures make it even more difficult for agencies to be effective.

It's easy to see why some government systems develop this kind of reactive rather than proactive approach to their work, despite their best intentions. As I noted in Chapter 2, most children come to the attention of the child welfare system due to neglect—most often due to poverty—rather than abuse. And research shows that separating families for any reason, even for a short time, can create lasting trauma for children.[3] It would be most helpful to connect these families to supportive services at the first sign of trouble, rather than waiting until a child has been hungry or homeless for months and then removing them from their parents because their basic needs aren't being met.

It would also be the cost-effective approach. The federal government funds states between $4,100 and $33,000 per child for foster care.[4] By contrast, the policy research institute Chapin Hall found that every additional $1,000 that a state spent on public benefit programs led to a 7.7 percent decrease in child maltreatment reports and foster care placements a month after families received the payment.[5] In other words, the amount of money it takes to remove children from their homes could be used, with much less harm to children, to stabilize their families.

Based on this insight and other research, there are agencies across the country trying to operate differently. Thriving Families, Safer Children is a first-of-its-kind initiative that includes child welfare agencies in twenty-two states. It has been supported by a range of partners, including Casey Family Programs, Prevent Child Abuse America, the Annie E. Casey Foundation, the National Center for Injury Prevention and Control at the Centers for Disease Control and Prevention, and the Administration for Children and Families.[6]

The purpose of Thriving Families is to help child protection systems move from the traditional, reactive approach to proactively support child and family well-being as a way to prevent child maltreatment and unnecessary family separation.[7] The effort aims to keep families out of the child welfare system by building strong community support networks and shifting government resources to offer a range of preventive services. This approach builds on the assets that families have while addressing any challenges they face.

One of the unique features of the Thriving Families effort is that it includes a range of community stakeholders like families who have been involved in the child welfare system (often referred to as people with lived expertise). The wisdom that comes from their experiences helps the participating agencies go beyond the theoretical to understand what is needed to meet the unique needs of families and promote the conditions to help them thrive.[8] As I will discuss in subsequent chapters, this approach of engaging families in solutions is rare but desperately needed.

Moreover, prevention isn't just needed in child welfare systems.

It is critically important for agencies to think proactively about every aspect of children's lives.

For example, the city of Memphis launched a youth survey asking young people for feedback on the kinds of programs and services they want and need.[9] When it comes to youth involved in the justice system, a proactive approach means thinking through options other than incarceration. In Lucas County, Ohio, and several other cities, officials hold a "stakeholder meeting," which often includes a young person and their family, to explore every alternative to putting a young person in a facility.[10]

At the Annie E. Casey Foundation, we have supported the implementation of systems in high schools that use readily available data to alert teachers and administrators to students who are at risk of dropping out. A key benefit of these systems is that they give educators helpful early indications of what to look for amid the mountains of data about students.

In other areas of child well-being, an effective ecosystem might include school lunch programs that ensure kids don't have to try to make it through the school day hungry; early health screenings to make sure they don't need glasses or have learning differences; or social-emotional programs that help kids learn how to manage their emotions productively to reduce depression and anxiety. While there are many other examples of prevention work in areas of child well-being, this approach is not common practice.

As I will discuss next, one critical way that agencies can understand where prevention resources are most needed is simply by talking with the families they seek to serve.

Engaging Customers in the Solutions

In business, it is common practice to talk to and get feedback from customers. You may be overwhelmed, as I have been, with repeated attempts by businesses to collect our feedback on everything from the purchase of a bucket of paint at the hardware store to impressions of customer service at one's last dental appointment. We even see a cleanliness survey these days in public restrooms. Why so many requests for input? This feedback loop is used to help their product, customer, and marketing teams understand where there is room for improvement so they can compete for our business.

Young people don't have governments competing to give them public services. But given how essential government services are to the success of youth and their families, one would assume governments would seek feedback and assess how they are doing in this vital role. However, while agency personnel frequently report on their performance to their leaders and legislators, they typically seek little feedback or engagement with the children, youth, and families who are their clients.

From Casey's decades of experience working with public systems, there are several reasons for this disconnect. One is fundamentally logistical: Agency staff are completing their work during the day when young people are in school and their parents are at work, making those engagement opportunities difficult. Also, agency staff typically don't receive training or have the capacity to engage families effectively. And agency staff are often overwhelmed with their workloads and focused on meeting reporting requirements. No matter which one of these reasons, it remains that many agencies are serving adolescents and their families without the benefit of their insights and ideas or a deep understanding of their experiences, culture, and values.

We have learned in our work that there is a tremendous amount to be gained by seeking feedback and insight from adolescents who are being served by a government agency. At the Foundation, we have found their input essential and invaluable in designing our youth strategies in our partnerships with public agencies. As I mentioned earlier, feedback from young people helped us identify the importance of basic needs, which is now one of five key priorities for our work. Adults have barriers to engaging youth in creating solutions, such as limited time, the preparation needed, and the assumptions adults often hold about young people. It takes an open mind and deliberate effort to pursue this approach.

I saw an example of a complex system deeply committed to prevention that put people at the forefront when I visited some nonprofits in Alaska on a learning tour. One stop was the Alaska Native Medical Center, one of several health care sites throughout the state that serve Alaska Native and American Indian people. At the center, they call the patients customer-owners. Providers paired the latest medical technologies with traditional native healing practices to ensure that their patient-customers received the care they both wanted and needed to be well.

The center had a traditional healing clinic where tribal doctors offered energy therapy, prayer, and dance. These tribal doctors are certified by an elder advisory council to ensure that their ancient practices continue through generations. While tribal doctors may provide recommendations for traditional medicine, the customer-owner must discuss those recommendations with their primary care physician to make sure they are compatible with the other medications they are taking. It was an example of modern medicine working in concert with ancient medicine in a way that was wholly owned and directed by the patient. Despite this being a big medical system, the focus was on people rather than compliance. Under this approach, the medical center has received an evidence-based practice award and recognition for improving health outcomes, all while centering the voices and experiences of Alaska Native and American Indian people.[11]

I'll share another example from my hometown of Atlanta. For nearly two decades, the Casey Foundation has been helping to redevelop a thirty-one-acre site on the city's south side, now called Pittsburgh Yards®.[12] The property sits in a majority-Black neighborhood with a long history of disinvestment, poverty, and displacement. In the past, either residents were ignored or, when people came in to offer help, they did it without consulting the community first. So, when Casey arrived, residents were understandably wary of another organization coming in. I didn't blame them. So many of the places I grew up going to in Atlanta are unrecognizable from all of the gentrification.

Casey hosted listening sessions where community members talked about the need for living wage jobs and better amenities. We held educational training and showed community members step-by-step how to analyze a market study to identify the best uses for the land. Then, based on that feedback, Casey collaborated with the community to develop a plan for the site to be an industrial hub with workspaces for entrepreneurs, manufacturing, and commercial uses.

Even after construction started, community members continued to play a key role in shaping the project through monthly engagement meetings, work groups, and other volunteer opportunities. They helped identify a property management firm and local artists to beautify the space. Residents also named several buildings and streets throughout the development. And residents continue to play a role influencing the programming that happens at the site and the use of the greenspace.

By involving residents from the start, the development team has been able to address a lot of the fear and skepticism and replace it with buy-in and trust. As a result, the community has come to see the project as an addition to—and an investment in—their history and strengths, rather than something to push them out.

In work across the Casey Foundation's areas of investment, we have seen time and time again how engaging young people simply leads to better outcomes.

In Chapter 5, I mentioned the SOUL Family framework, a concept developed by young people that provides options that jurisdictions can deploy to allow young people in foster care to form a legal attachment to nonrelatives when they are at risk of aging out of the system at eighteen or twenty-one. The state of Kansas passed legislation to adopt key elements of the approach, and several young people are pursuing this route to permanency with their chosen family.

For the world of work and career, young people who participated in our LEAP initiative have helped employers better understand how to recruit, train, and retain younger workers.

In our juvenile justice work, we have seen positive results and real system reform when young people can be engaged in positive ways to help shape their future.

In short, when young people are consulted or engaged in designing the services they will use, they can support solutions that reflect their diverse experiences and needs. Without this, we risk perpetuating inequities through systems that affect youth today and in the future.

Serving Young People as a Part of Families

There is an inherent tension for young people as they navigate different systems on the way to adulthood. On the one hand, this is a stage of life when building independence and exploring the world on your own is important. Social bonds outside of the family are becoming more important than the family unit, as I discussed in Chapter 1. At the same time, adolescents need to be connected with their parents and other supportive adults who can support young people as their executive functioning grows and develops.

Young people need to know that there are adults who care about them—whether that is from within families, within a closely connected community, or in programs that serve young people.[13]

Yet in the same way that too many public agencies fail to engage young people themselves in improving the services and supports to help them succeed, they also often fail to sufficiently engage the families. As family is the support system closest to a young person, this constitutes a missed opportunity to leverage the trust and assets they bring to help young people cross the bridge to adulthood.

In the case of a young person on probation, I have discussed in a previous chapter the approach of bringing families into the process of planning for a young person's time on probation. Under this engage-the-family planning model, the probation officer would work to build a relationship with the young person and the family members and other supporting adults in their lives.[14] Probation officers look to family members for their expert insight into the young person. The model is designed to move away from the idea that young people involved in juvenile justice are broken and in need of fixing, and to transform the monitoring that is built into a probation officer's job to include building a relationship with the adolescent. This approach involves families from the beginning through meetings facilitated by a third party, typically a community-based organization, with all parties participating as equal members of a young person's team.[15]

Similar strategies have been effective in child welfare, particularly when extended families are engaged to support parents who might be struggling. Trying to decide whether a child should be separated from their parents or caregivers to prevent abuse and neglect is perhaps the most consequential decision child welfare workers make. We want to make sure that children are cared for and free from harm, but removing a child from his or her home is among the most traumatic experiences in their lives given the attachment children have to their caregivers, even if those adults are struggling.

For decades, the Annie E. Casey Foundation has encouraged agencies to use an approach called Team Decision Making™ (TDM) that we developed to help workers when facing this difficult choice. TDM, which the California Evidence-Based Clearinghouse has found to have promising evidence,[16] helps child welfare agencies make the most informed decisions possible.

How it works: A Team Decision Making meeting happens every time a safety concern arises about a child, and before a child is separated from their caregivers. The meetings are led by a trained facilitator and include parents, children, agency staff, family members, and community members who know the family. The goal is to talk about safety risks to the child, family strengths, and any other characteristics of resilience in the support system to develop a consensus-based plan and recommendations for moving forward.

The Important Role of Policymakers

Elected officials set the policies and approve the funding that enable public systems to operate. When I refer to policymakers, I mean elected officials from all political parties and at all levels of government—local, state, and federal—who create and pass laws, regulations, ordinances, and rulings.

Policymakers have an important part to play in making sure that other entities in the ecosystem have what they need to do their best work. They have the power to implement policies and fund programs to ensure quality education for young people from preschool to college. For health care, policies approved by lawmakers can expand access to care and insurance coverage. For employment and economic opportunities, policymakers can support the creation of job training and apprenticeship programs with public dollars. Public investments and zoning regulations approved by officials affect the location, quantity, and affordability of housing for families. And the amount of money that goes toward social services is critical. Social safety net programs provide crucial support to almost 100 million people experiencing economic hardship.[17] Nearly half of all U.S. children participate in a safety net program.[18]

A study on how state legislators make decisions on education policy found these three top factors: fiscal impact, the trust of the people providing the information and counsel, and constituents.[19] That means that adolescents have the power to be influential by voicing their opinions on policy decisions, like through public testimony.[20] We have seen many times how the stories and advocacy of young people inspire and inform the work of public officials. But we've also seen how public outcry can outweigh the youth perspective.

This is a phenomenon that we see all the time. One child death in state care—which should not happen—now means that more children are removed from homes as a precaution. Or a heinous crime is committed by a single young person, and public officials declare a "tough on crime" stance that seeks to lock up more young people under harsher penalties. Instead of looking carefully at the situation, there is a shift toward taking extreme action to prevent a repeat in the future.

The crimes are horrendous, real harm has occurred, and the pain and desire for safety and justice is real. These reactive policies and practices may feel safe in the short term. We see a terrible headline about a young person committing a crime, and leaders implement legislation to lock more kids up thinking that will keep people safe. But decades of research shows that that doesn't work. In fact, there is evidence that for every day that youth are incarcerated, they are more likely to be rearrested.[21] The community is no safer; high rates of youth incarceration do not improve public safety, but they do lead to long-term harm to young people's physical and mental health. We can't let emotions outweigh what research and data tell us are the best approaches to address complex issues like child abuse and public safety. Especially in these times of crisis, we need data-informed decision-making.

Given that, the most important shift for policymakers to make is to recognize that they have a critically important role to play in the lives of young people. They can inhabit that role by, for example, creating some of the enabling mechanisms for public agencies to take up the shifts recommended in this chapter. And when they do, the results can produce powerful outcomes. In Minneapolis, the Youth Coordinating Board—a policy-focused partnership between the city and county government, schools, and the city's parks and recreation department—developed a Youth Master Plan that includes common goals, more after-school opportunities, and improved early childhood education.[22] Their recommendations included more youth participation on municipal boards and city council commissions, paving the way for an opportunity for young people and legislators to engage with each other on issues affecting them.[23]

I've highlighted quite a few things that public agencies can do to better support adolescents: move further upstream to intervene before problems happen, work toward solutions with a young person's family, and engage young people in developing solutions. But government actors are not alone in needing to strengthen their approach to helping young people thrive. Employers are another key group whose investment in the future and talents of young people matters—both to the young people and to employers' ability to sustain a strong pool of talent for the next generation.

Employers must take a role in getting young people ready to transition into the workforce. It's true that they invest in young people through the wages paid. But employers have an opportunity to understand the importance of young people in multiple ways, such as consumers and as parents who need reliable childcare. As the next generation of workers, customers, and community leaders, adolescents need employers to engage with them to succeed into adulthood.

11

Employers

In high school, I was accepted into a competitive program that prepared youth for careers in corporate America. INROADS guaranteed an internship for all four years of college, access to mentors, and weekly Saturday training on invaluable workplace soft skills like business etiquette and making effective presentations. INROADS interns also had priority for permanent jobs at their companies after college graduation.

As a student at the University of Virginia majoring in business, I had an INROADS internship every summer at a technology company in Atlanta. I worked in their sales, finance, and legal departments. I attended meetings, researched case law, and produced reports. During the academic year, an INROADS mentor checked in on me monthly.

As a young person still learning and finding her way, INROADS was one of my most formative and encouraging work experiences. I learned new skills, was trained by professionals, experienced business work culture, met numerous mentors, and contributed new ideas. I wish all young people could have these kinds of formative experiences, not just a select few.

I went on to law school so I didn't end up working at the technology company after graduation. But decades later when I joined UPS, I was a part of INROADS again—this time as a mentor. I remember explaining UPS culture to my first intern, Nikki, just like others had done years before for me. Nikki was capable and eager to work in our department and learn about the work world. After her internship, Nikki went to law school. Today, she is a high-ranking tax attorney at CSX.

My career is now in philanthropy, but I spent many years working in the business world. I believe my success in corporate America and my role as Casey's CEO are connected to the foundation of skills and relationships I developed during internship experiences when I was a teenager and a young adult.

The employers who participated in the INROADS program sent a signal through their participation—they cared about young people as the country's future talent. Through the program, the employers created a tangible pathway to a good job at their respective companies.

My INROADS experience is one example of the role employers can play in ensuring that young people make the transition from school to work. Employers can help young people learn and develop the skills that are needed in the workplace. Employers also provide jobs that facilitate a young person's path to economic stability and empowerment.

Early jobs help young people explore their career interests. This allows them to gain valuable work experience in a supportive environment that can recognize their talents and needs as new workers.

These early work experiences also help support young people as they mature and work toward becoming self-sufficient adults. Early employment opportunities give young people the perspectives and skills that can ease their path toward careers. When combined with a postsecondary degree and work-based, positive relationships with adults, these opportunities lay the foundation for the future success of young people in work.[1]

Apprenticeships are a particularly effective model. In a 2016 study by the U.S. Department of Commerce on the effectiveness of apprenticeships, one business in the study, Siemens, described receiving a 50 percent rate of return from their apprenticeship program at one North Carolina plant that makes generators for electric utilities and repairs on those products. One year of the additional capacity generated by the program nearly canceled out the cost of the program itself.

I believe something else can help employers engage young people more successfully: a deeper understanding and acknowledgment of adolescent brain science. Understanding how the adolescent brain works and what young people need to be successful can provide useful insight for organizations seeking to smooth the transition for young people from education to the workplace.

As I discussed in Chapter 1, the teenage brain craves new experiences and is adaptable and ready to learn.[2] It's essential for employers to understand that young adults are more used to classrooms than boardrooms, and their executive functioning is still developing. Still, through innovative partnerships, employers can provide young people with enriching early work opportunities. At the same time, it is vital to align with the business goals of private employers to maximize profits. These goals are not necessarily at odds; for companies to remain viable, they need access to talented employees and a thriving future customer base. Young people serve as both. There are examples of innovative partnerships happening around the country that are redefining what it looks like for employers to support young people in their early work experiences.

The Role of Employers

Employers produce goods and services that contribute to our economy and overall economic success. As such, they are influential institutions in communities that have an important role to play in the lives of young people entering adulthood. Because of their role in society and their economic power, the work of employers intersects with each of the Thrive by 25 areas—basic needs, permanent connections, education and credentials, financial stability, and community and youth leadership—in clear ways.

Employers can take many forms: There is the for-profit business sector; the government, which is a large employer; and the nonprofit social sector, which includes hospitals and schools. The business sector exists alongside the government and the social sector. These sectors work together as important entities in society that affect the lives of all of us, including young people.

As someone who spent decades working in the business world, I know that it is not seamless for young people to gain entry into work and challenges await them once they do.

First is the challenge of supporting youth with fundamental skills even as the requirements and settings for work are changing so rapidly. Multiple pressures and demands on employers would seem to make maximizing output the top priority over supporting the next generation of workers. Plus, the increased use of technology in the workplace means that the pace of business innovation is much faster than decades ago. As technology reshapes business strategy and outputs, it also has transformed how young people seek out and experience their earliest jobs.

The COVID-19 pandemic required a rapid shift to virtual work opportunities. While many employers have returned to in-person operations, about half of U.S. workers in remote-capable jobs work in a hybrid model, while one-quarter work exclusively remote.[3] This shift is creating opportunities for virtual internships and has broadened the kinds of roles that are available to young people, like data science and cybersecurity.[4]

New technology requires new skills from employees. By 2027, more than 40 percent of workers' core skills will have to change because technology is moving faster than employers can train their employees.[5] The three skills most in demand all pertain to mindset and reflect the shifting workplace, requiring employees who are resilient and can think analytically and creatively.[6] Young people will need to cultivate these in-demand skills in their early work experiences.

Reconnecting Young People to Work

Millions of young people ages sixteen to twenty-four in the United States are not in school, are without college degrees, and have little work experience. These young people are commonly referred to as opportunity youth, or disconnected youth. They live in all types of communities—urban, suburban, and rural—and come from a variety of family backgrounds. Some of the young people most likely to become disconnected include youth who have experienced foster care or become involved in the juvenile justice system. As of 2022, at least 11 percent of young people ages sixteen to twenty-four, or nearly 4.35 million adolescents and young adults, were not in school or working.[7]

Policymakers and practitioners have been working for decades to connect young people who are not in school or working to the employment system. The solutions have ranged from summer youth employment programs to the U.S. Department of Labor's YouthBuild pre-apprenticeship program[8] to the Neighborhood Youth Corps of the 1960s.[9] These programs have had some successes, but many young people still lack opportunity and more programs are needed to support them.

We should be concerned about the job prospects for these young people, and for many others who never have the opportunity to earn family-sustaining wages. In 2022, 42 percent of U.S. households were struggling to make ends meet; this includes households with income below the federal poverty line, and households that have limited assets and constraints on their income while also being employed.[10] As young people enter and stay in the workforce, they need to work for employers that pay them a wage where they can meet their basic needs. This is less about a particular job title and more about young people working and being able to take care of themselves with the money they earn from work. I believe it takes a multifaceted approach to connect young people to education and employment opportunities that will benefit employers while also allowing young people to build the personal and professional skills that can give them and their families economic stability.

Financial stability is key for young people to have success through work to build their lives. For young people coming out of foster care, financial support can make the difference in how they are able to take care of themselves and show up for work. Through the Casey Foundation's Jim Casey Youth Opportunities Initiative®, young people can participate in the Opportunity Passport® program, which helps young people leaving foster care get help to build financial stability. The program provides them with financial education, a savings account with matching funds, and tools to support their future goals such as buying a car or going to college. This program, a partnership between local foster care agencies, nonprofits, philanthropy, and financial institutions, is designed to give these young adults the financial skills and resources they need to be self-sufficient and thrive long term.[11]

Programs like this, and others, make it clear that no system or sector can do it alone, and a range of organizations and agencies must play an important role. Systems including workforce development, K–12 schools, career and technical education, higher education, child welfare, juvenile justice, and community development must coordinate and connect their efforts. To get some or even all of these systems on the same page would require a wholesale shift in how we serve young people.

What Young Workers Need
Several things that employers do right now make it more difficult for young workers, especially those who have been disconnected, to succeed in the workplace. Too many employers either don't think about setting up the kinds of supportive structures needed to help young people reach their full potential, or they don't know how.

In my role at Casey, I've talked with employers, visited

apprenticeships and other innovative programs, and read research on creating optimal working conditions for young people. I've learned what many workplaces look like now when they are not set up to serve young people and what needs to change.

Many workplaces have a one-size-fits-all approach to recruiting and managing their talent. Younger employees are still developing executive functioning skills so they can handle the basics of the job. The recruiting process may not be sufficiently developed to ensure the young person's skills and strengths are a good match for the job. Onboarding into a new role must be tailored to adolescents who need and want coaching and skill-building assistance in the workplace. This could be in the form of a work mentor, more frequent check-ins than tenured staff, or other support.

Many employers have designed their compensation and benefits to meet the needs of older, not younger, workers. For lower-income workers, the path to increased compensation is unclear. As they enter full-time positions, many younger workers start in low-wage jobs, and it can be difficult for them to step out of those to develop the skills or credentials they need for higher-paying work. As for internships, many are still unpaid, which privileges higher-income students who don't have an urgent need to make money. Employers need to have pay and benefits that match the needs of younger workers; examples include offering childcare benefits and tuition reimbursement. Even as employers may feel financial pressure to provide these benefits, they can also invest in young talent by creating a workplace with a sense of purpose and meaning, values that some young workers say they care about more than wages.[12]

Scheduling instability is another challenge that young people increasingly face.[13] Last-minute changes, which employers may make to save on costs or respond to business needs, can affect a young worker's ability to balance school, family, and work. They tend to have fewer resources and flexibility to respond to these changes, causing ripple effects in many aspects of their lives.

Many employers don't have the partnerships with educational institutions or workforce training providers that would ensure that skills young people are developing match open roles. Too often there is a mismatch between how education prepares young people for work and what young people know how to do in a workplace. The right partnerships can eliminate this gap and strike a balance between an employer's needs and a young person's interests, preparation, and learning—hopefully to increase a youth's engagement and successful employment.

One example is the Collaborative of Leaders in Academia and Business (CoLAB), based near Washington, D.C. Through CoLAB's Employer Signaling System (ESS), the group combines labor market data with employer feedback to develop a list of the knowledge, skills, abilities, and credentials needed for entry-level IT jobs in the region so that high school educators can use those criteria to teach and prepare their students for those jobs.[14] Employers need to develop these kinds of partnerships that will give them this insight into the incoming workforce.

Too many employers are waiting for young people to graduate and find their way to them, instead of creating innovative pathways that will lead to on-ramps into their profession, like apprenticeships. Fortunately, new models that engage more young people in work-based learning are gaining traction. We've encountered and developed several of these partnerships through our work at the Casey Foundation, and I'll describe a few.

1.

In Albuquerque, New Mexico, a nonprofit called Future Focused Education enables high school students to gain real-world experience by completing paid internships with a variety of local employers—many of them small businesses. The internship program, X3, is open to high school and early college students. These young people work twelve hours a week for thirteen weeks, learning on-the-job skills under the supervision of a mentor.

The program has three elements. First, students earn a stipend that would likely replace the minimum wage jobs they might otherwise take to support their families. Second, they are treated like actual work colleagues and complete needed work, which allows the young people to develop skills that they can include on their resumes. Finally, they get to increase their network by connecting with and being mentored by professionals in the field. These connections are especially vital for students without a large network or a significant amount of community relationships.[15]

On the employer side, participating employers attend training where they can learn about the services that are in place to support the intern. They are also assigned a coach. The program addresses common concerns like how to create an optimal experience, understanding the kind of work assignments interns can complete, and how to address common issues for new workers like arriving late or being dressed inappropriately.[16]

X3 mentor Delcie Dobrovolny described the valuable experiences of two different students who were both interns at their architecture firm Equiterra Regenerative Design. Dobrovolny said one student learned that she didn't want to be an architect because the internship taught her that she didn't enjoy the work. From her perspective, this was a valuable revelation. The second intern was able to learn the architecture software within two weeks; after a month, the intern was creating work that was billable to clients. Dobrovolny said she was surprised that the intern learned the software much faster than an adult employee coming from a graduate program.[17]

The X3 program is popular and growing. During the 2023–24 school year, Future Focused Education provided 401 high school students with paid internships at ninety-six private, public, and nonprofit employers across the state.[18]

Another employer in the X3 program, the University of New

Mexico Hospital, places student interns alongside hospital staff where they also interact with patients. The effort has increased the number of students interested in going into the health care industry. The project is also helping the University of New Mexico Hospital create a new pipeline of workers following significant employment gaps from retirements.[19] This example shows the expanded ability of employers to tap new sources of talent and reach talented workers they might not otherwise have considered. The success of the program has led UNMH to ask Future Focused Education to help source its workforce pipeline.[20]

Alli Sillas, director of social-emotional learning and well-being for Future Focused Education, has seen the program help students change. "Their ability to dream, and believe that they belong in the community and that they have a place somewhere where their greatness can shine."[21] Isn't this the kind of experience we want for all young people?

2.

YouthBuild Philadelphia provides training and coaching to frontline supervisors at local employers—including a grocery store, coffee shop, and clothing retailer—so that they can better support young workers. Participating employers have made changes to employment practices, including adjusting work hours and hiring practices. This allowed cashiers to get the work hours they want and need, eliminating the scheduling and income unpredictability that affects many young workers. Employers also made changes like making shifts longer, having regular check-ins with frontline staff, and demonstrating empathy when mistakes occur. While other workforce providers may do similar work, YouthBuild created internal structures like dedicated staff to support this work.

3.

The Partnership to Advance Youth Apprenticeship (PAYA) is a multi-stakeholder initiative that assists organizations around the country in developing youth apprenticeship programs. The initiative has outlined five principles of high-quality apprenticeships:

1. They are career oriented. Young people who participate do real-life work as employees, and the companies who participate develop a structured experience with educators so that students can learn.
2. They are equitable. Students who have historically been denied opportunities because of their gender, income, disability, or race must have access to the opportunity. That means that the apprenticeship programs cannot be geared to just the most privileged students.
3. They are portable. The experience of a student apprenticeship participant must count toward a college degree or another credential past high school, through earning credit or a certification.
4. They must be adaptable. While employers can be specialized, they must provide an opportunity where student participants can develop broad and transferable skills.
5. They must be accountable. There are multiple actors in an apprenticeship program experience—the student, employer, and program support—and each one of them must adhere to their role and be accountable for it.[22]

The Partnership to Advance Youth Apprenticeship provides intensive support and funding to fourteen partnerships across the country that are working to create high-quality youth apprenticeship opportunities for high school students. According to New

America, a nonprofit that oversees PAYA, these grantees matched more than 2,400 youth apprentices with 380 employers between 2023 and 2024. Young people who completed their apprenticeships earned an average annual salary of $53,996.

Coda: The Business Case for Wraparound Support

Any discussion about what employers can do to facilitate youth and young adult success is incomplete without mentioning childcare, as many young people entering the workforce are also parents. There were 3.4 million children in the United States living with parents ages eighteen to twenty-four in 2018.[23] These young parents need financial stability and high-quality, affordable childcare to be the best employee they can be, especially when they are in an earlier period of their career and likely earning less money. Also, we know from adolescent brain science that young parents are at a point where they are still growing and developing. These "two open windows" of development,[24] parent and child, mean that support for young parents with childcare is especially critical at a time when they may be balancing parenting and employment with finishing school. In addition to ensuring parents can work, high-quality early care has been proven to provide children with enhanced social and emotional skills, stronger school readiness, and a solid foundation for future learning and success in life.[25]

There is a cost to insufficient childcare, and it affects not just an individual family but other employees in the workplace and the overall business. Businesses lose an estimated $1,640 per working parent in reduced revenue and extra hiring costs due to childcare challenges. In total, the average burden on businesses from unreliable and insufficient childcare is $23 billion.[26]

Many employers provide health benefits to their employees and already understand the business case for a strong employee benefits package. But not enough seek to help employees resolve the critical issue of childcare that would enable them to work. Struggling to find childcare can throw a wrench in a caregiver's life—leaving work early, showing up late, or missing days altogether. Even worse, about 1 in 4 parents have lost their jobs because of these challenges.[27] It's a vicious cycle: Without childcare, they lose their income, which makes it even harder to afford the care they need to get back on their feet.

Childcare would help all employees—but is especially helpful for younger workers who are balancing work, parenting, and school. These young workers are still developing and need more support. Even if they don't provide on-site childcare or a stipend, employers have an opportunity to advocate for the kinds of wraparound support that young workers need, which can benefit their entire workforce. It is essential for employers to actively engage in supporting adolescents in all the ways that they need—their investment benefits the individual employee while also contributing to a skilled and capable workforce for the future.

12

The Social Sector

United Way. 4-H. Big Brothers Big Sisters of America. YMCA. Girl Scouts of the USA. Boys & Girls Clubs of America.

These national organizations serve millions of youth and their families every day. They are household names and part of the fabric of communities across the country. The efforts of these groups, along with lesser-known organizations working at the local level, reflect the compassion and caring spirit of millions of Americans to help others in their community. Half of all Americans donate to charity, and nearly a quarter volunteer each year.[1] This generosity, and the nonprofit infrastructure that supports it, constitutes one of the most widespread and important tools we have to help young people succeed.

Nonprofits: Facts and History

The U.S. social sector is made up of organizations determined by the IRS to serve one of these purposes: charitable, religious, educational, scientific, literary, testing for public safety, fostering amateur sports competition, or preventing cruelty to children or animals. As a result, these organizations are exempt from many forms of taxation and are thus often referred to as "tax-exempt organizations" or described by the section of the tax code—501(c)(3)—that provides this exemption. The common thread that runs through these kinds of organizations and their leaders is this: Their work supports a public good or social mission through private actions outside of government.[2]

Philanthropy, the area I work in, is a part of the social sector. It involves providing grants and resources to people, organizations, and issues that support and improve the well-being of individuals and society as a whole. While the social sector is funded through earned revenue, public dollars, individual generosity, and corporate contributions, foundations like ours have funds of varying sizes created to make charitable donations. The Annie E. Casey Foundation, for example, is a philanthropic organization focused on building a brighter future for children, youth, families, and communities in the United States.

Although philanthropy is a niche of the social sector, the scale of its giving can have an outsized impact. For example, the Robert Wood Johnson Foundation, together with many grantees and partners, chose to tackle the issue of tobacco addiction and its impact on the lives of smokers and those around them.[3] This sustained effort over many decades supported policy advocacy that led to smoke-free indoor air laws and new federal tobacco regulations that have saved an estimated 8 million lives.[4]

Nonprofit organizations are a deeply rooted reflection of American creativity, altruism, and entrepreneurial innovation. Individuals like businessmen John D. Rockefeller and Andrew Carnegie amassed significant fortunes through the 1800s and used their wealth to create institutions such as libraries and museums for public benefit. In the 1960s, the government began to contract with nonprofits to provide services and there was increased advocacy for civil rights, the environment, and other social issues. Both factors led the nonprofit sector to grow.[5]

Today, there are nearly 2 million nonprofits in the United States,[6] including more than 126,000 private foundations. The vast majority of nonprofits, 88 percent, have budgets smaller than $500,000, are community-based, and serve local needs.[7] About 12.5 million people are employed by nonprofits, roughly 10.2 percent of the private-sector workforce.[8]

Nonprofits play a critical role in the ecosystem of our society, as well as the ecosystem for youth. The government is obligated to act and provide certain services based on the law. Private companies sell goods to consumers at a profit according to their articles of incorporation. But what if you don't qualify for a certain government program? Or what if you don't have the financial resources to purchase what you need from a private source? That's where nonprofits step in. Name an issue and a nonprofit likely exists to address it.

Through their direct and contracted services, nonprofits address unmet needs and offer services in education, mental and physical health, arts and culture, and religion—filling service gaps between government and for-profit businesses. Nonprofits are a critical piece of the support system that undergirds adolescents, and they are a powerful player in the ability of young people to thrive into adulthood.

Helping Young People Cross the Bridge

While nonprofits are not a monolith, many of them provide young people with resources, opportunities, and safe spaces for support that can significantly influence personal development and professional prospects. These kinds of organizations in many instances are a lifeline for youth, offering a range of services that help them navigate the complexities of the journey to adulthood.

Although these kinds of nonprofits can play this transformative role in the lives of young people, the most effective nonprofits, in my view, do not operate to impose solutions or rescue young people from their circumstances. Instead, these organizations offer young people tools, support, and the opportunity to navigate their path. This approach respects the agency and individuality of young people, fostering their growth and resilience.

To meet basic needs, nonprofits offer programs and services directly to young people so they can have access to necessities such as food, clean clothes, and a safe place to live. These efforts provide essential services and support that allow the adolescent to focus on other aspects of their development, like school and making and maintaining friendships. By meeting these basic needs, nonprofits help families create a secure environment in which young people can thrive and pursue their goals.

Establishing permanent, supportive relationships with caring adults is critical for young people's emotional and social development. Specialized nonprofits partner with child welfare agencies to identify and train foster and adoptive parents who serve as temporary or long-term families for youth in foster care. More generally, nonprofits can facilitate connections between youth and adults through programs like Big Brothers Big Sisters of America, a nationally known mentoring organization. Through this range of efforts, young people have the opportunity to develop trusting relationships with adults who can offer guidance, listen, and support young people as they share their experiences and challenges.

As seen in the Thread example in Chapter 5, nonprofits can play a powerful role in helping young people—especially students in need of extra support—complete their education and prepare for future careers. Nonprofits do this through charter schools, tutoring services, education enrichment, internships, and apprenticeships that offer exposure to college and careers, and training and certification programs. Many nonprofit programs aim to support young people in achieving their educational and professional goals. These organizations empower young people to take charge of their futures and build the skills and confidence needed to succeed on their terms.

Achieving financial stability is a crucial aspect of transitioning to adulthood. Nonprofits assist in this area by offering job training, internships, and financial literacy programs. They teach young people essential skills like budgeting, saving, and investing—providing the knowledge needed to manage finances effectively. These efforts are geared toward empowering young people to build a secure financial future as their executive functioning skills develop. Equipping young people with tools and skills enables them to make informed financial decisions and can foster their independence.

As for youth leadership, nonprofits also play a vital role in cultivating this quality in youth. They can offer programs that help young people develop skills in advocacy, public speaking, and community organizing. These kinds of programs encourage young people to take on policy challenges and advocate for themselves and their communities.

When this happens, young people develop a sense of agency in their lives and use that to advocate on behalf of others. This growing sense of civic responsibility can instill a lifelong understanding of ways they can be active participants in shaping their future and that of their communities. The goal is not to prescribe a specific path for activism but to support young people in finding their voice so they can make a difference. This approach respects the diverse perspectives and passions of young people, which allows them to pursue causes that matter to them.

The Call to Action for Nonprofits

There are four major ways that the social sector can refine its approaches and maximize its positive influence on the lives of young people. First, nonprofit organizations can tailor adolescent programming with their unique needs in mind. According to the National Institute on Out-of-School Time, adolescents take part in programs in a different way from younger children and need to have programs better matched to their needs.[9] For example, for programs that have a teen component, the physical space for teen programming needs to reflect their activities and interests because this affects how the youth interact in the space.[10] In other words, the design and layout—including the furniture and how it is arranged in a room—all matters to a young person.

Next, nonprofits and the foundations that fund them need to engage young people in co-designing programming that affects them. Just like a patient often knows best how to describe how they are feeling, young people should be asked to articulate what is not working and what they need instead. Take Baltimore's Promise collaborative, for example. It works to increase access to opportunity and to improve outcomes for the city's youth. A 2023 report led by Baltimore's Promise looked at how and where public and private funds for young people in Baltimore were spent. Its analysis revealed there were 2.3 times the number of opportunities for elementary school-aged children than for older youth (ages 19-24). In addition, it found that programming for older youth is largely limited to the summer months. Specifically, ninety-four percent of program sites and seventy percent of opportunities identified for older youth occurred during the summer. This leaves adolescents in Baltimore with very limited opportunities for positive engagement throughout the year.

Baltimore's Promise CEO Julia Baez said that studying the funding and where it goes shows how there needs to be sustained investment in young people into adulthood, which includes support for things like career readiness, financial literacy, mental health support, and housing services.[11]

In response to the disparities in funding by age group, Baltimore's Promise created an initiative, Youth Grantmakers, that puts young people squarely at the center. Youth Grantmakers are a group of young people ages seventeen to twenty-four who meet to award grants to organizations that provide programs and work with older youth. Working with an adult advisor from Baltimore's Promise, the youth committee determines the guidelines and goals for the grants. The young people also work with grantees during the grant period to help the recipients improve their efforts and make the grant more effective. The young people are trained and compensated for their work.

The 2024 grants, known collectively as "A Promise II BMORE: BMORE on Purpose," were used to support workforce and post-secondary employment programs for their peers. Through the more equitable distribution of opportunities, older youth and young adults were able to try new things, experience the feeling of accomplishment, gain new skills and certifications, and ultimately obtain jobs. By being engaged this way, the youth grant makers were motivated to continue their efforts and advocacy in service to their community. "My time as a Youth Grantmaker has taught me to keep fighting for Baltimore," said Camila Colero.[12]

Another powerful role nonprofits can play is to influence more positive narratives about the impact and potential of youth, especially in the communities where they work. Nonprofits are uniquely positioned to encourage leaders and the public to go beyond stereotypes when talking about young people because of their deep ties to communities, mission-driven focus, and the trust that they build through their service and advocacy.

Narrative change work is important because perception is reality and can lead to adverse consequences. Commonly held stereotypes about teenagers, for example, portray them as disinterested in education, work, and the world around them. But nonprofits that work with thousands of youth firsthand know that young people are motivated, want to succeed, and have big dreams for themselves, their future families, and their communities. Nonprofits can tell these stories and can support young people to tell their stories. Negative narratives close doors of opportunity to young people and lead adults to assume the worst or avoid engaging them, creating a vicious cycle at the time young people are forming their identities and concepts of themselves. A strong youth ecosystem sends the consistent, affirming, and encouraging message that youth are worthy of investment, have valuable contributions and strengths, and are capable of succeeding.

According to an internal media scan Casey commissioned in 2024, the public conversation around youth is very much focused on deficits—like crime, gun violence, and mental health issues. These messages are not at all in line with how young people describe themselves. They're talking about the economy and wanting to work. They talked about their communities, their homes, and their families. And they talked about their educational goals.

We do young people—and ourselves—no service with negative stories and attitudes. It becomes a self-fulfilling prophecy. If we want young people to thrive—and our country to prosper—then it's time we tell a new story about them. That story is rightly full of hope and potential and articulates the role we all must play to support their success.

To do that, we need to first get adults—including parents, policymakers, and employers—to appreciate the promise of adolescence as reflected in the data and research. The experiences a young person has and the opportunities they have to try new things and grow during this time have a marked effect on their future trajectory (and ours in community with them). We must also focus the narrative on what young people say they need to thrive—basic needs, like food and housing; caring relationships with adults; education and employment opportunities; a sense of belonging.

Finally, let's lift up the aspirations we know young people have for themselves—to work, to learn, to build skills, and to become self-sufficient. Not just for them, and not just because it's the right thing to do. But because when young people thrive, our communities thrive. The more we can help people to embrace that sense of shared responsibility, the better we will all be. Nonprofits are perfectly positioned to play this role and to champion these efforts.

To highlight this more accurate view of young people, the Boys & Girls Clubs of America runs programs that show adolescents as inspiring, uplifting their communications and creating positive change. Its annual youth leadership recognition program invites more than 3,600 local clubs to select one young club member as Youth of the Year, who goes on to compete at the city, regional, and ultimately national level.

The National Youth of the Year is a highly prized opportunity for a young person to serve as an ambassador for other young people. The winner is named national teen spokesperson for the nonprofit, representing more than 3.6 million youth who are members of the Boys & Girls Clubs and young people in general.[13] I have served as a judge for this event and I was blown away by the accomplishments, presence, and ambition of every applicant.

The Call to Action for Philanthropy

Philanthropy, in the monetary sense, refers to the act of donating money, resources, or time to charitable causes or organizations with the aim of improving societal well-being and addressing issues such as poverty, education, health care, or the environment. It often seeks to use the money to address root causes of problems so that the change can be longer lasting.

As a sector, philanthropy has the unique ability to bring together diverse stakeholders and to make investments for systemic and long-term change. To best support adolescents on the journey to adulthood, philanthropy can invest in bringing nonprofits, employers, governments, and communities together to create solutions that address the multiple needs of young people. Understanding young people as a unique population with specific needs can create more effective, holistic solutions than just considering them through the lens of an individual issue.

In addition, philanthropy can support successful and effective nonprofits in replicating their programs so that more young people can be served. At Casey, we describe this as scale—the point when a program or policy reaches most and eventually all of the people it needs to reach. As nonprofits consider scaling their programs, they must consider things like the scope of need, how the program might need to be adapted for other participants, organizational capacity, and financial sustainability. It often takes many years or even decades to grow a program, which affects how quickly we can see changes in the desired outcomes.

By addressing critical needs, empowering youth through leadership programs, and advocating for systemic change, nonprofits play a transformative role in shaping adolescents in the journey to adulthood. Nonprofits make an invaluable contribution to young people and we must seek innovative ways to enhance their impact so that every young person that comes into contact with this sector has the chance to reach their full potential.

Because young people are not living one-dimensional lives, the best way for the government, employers, and the education and social sectors to make the greatest impact on the lives of young people is by collaborating and working together to identify and solve issues. With this kind of coordination, the infrastructure that supports young people and their path toward adulthood serves as a strong undergirding for their journey. Through a collective effort, we can build stronger, more resilient communities where all adolescents can flourish.

13

Coordination and Navigation

I have described each of the critical and distinct actors in the ecosystem that surrounds and supports adolescents. Sometimes these entities need help coming together. When they do, they form a unified and powerful support system much like a choir producing a beautiful, harmonious performance that is greater than the sum of its parts.

As these entities align, young people should be better able to navigate the fractured environment of resources and support they might need at various times. It is useless to have services, programs, and opportunities for young people if they cannot find them or have difficulty accessing them. Or if they aren't coordinated and young people can't figure out how to put the pieces together because they are provided by different sectors.

Some of the young people who are getting lost on their journey to adulthood would benefit from a more tightly woven network of services and support. While the journey to adulthood is an individual one where each adolescent has to go through a personal process of physical and emotional maturity, young people need our support to help them navigate through the options and barriers they confront—as their brains continue to develop and mature. In this chapter, I will discuss why and how the elements of the ecosystem need to align so that young people can more easily access the various services and supports that are available to them as they grow into adults.

One Adolescent, Many Systems

Young people rely on the sectors described in previous chapters to build and sustain their lives. They go to school, seek jobs, take part in programs and opportunities, and receive services from the ecosystem that surrounds them. But a young person is not experiencing each of those things one at a time. The ecosystem around them is in constant motion (or needs to be) to provide the best support for young people as they grow into adulthood. Young people access this support in different ways and at different times. But no one person puts all those pieces together for them.

Let me use the example of a young person at the end of high school who is making a transition to college. As young people plan for this transition, they have to figure out which colleges to apply to and comply with varying application requirements. Once accepted, most students must figure out how to pay for college, which includes completing the federal financial aid form, which is only available online and very complex. During that process, young people are engaging with the federal government that creates the form, with their parents or guardians to collect the information needed to complete the form, and perhaps even with a counselor or nonprofit program that is guiding and mentoring them through the application. And if they make it to campus, how does a young person know how to register for classes, find housing, or pick the right meal plan? These choices all require a higher level of executive function, and the young person is still maturing in that area. They are away from home, typically for the first time, and separated from consistent adult support. In some cases, some youth are in this new phase of their lives never having had consistent support. Either way, a young person finds themselves responsible for figuring out how to navigate many things at once including academic, financial, insurance, and housing concerns—not to mention the significant social transition. These are vital needs that will highly impact the young person's success in college if meeting them is a struggle.

Most adults struggle with this kind of executive functioning, referred to in popular culture as "adulting." As we know through brain science, adolescents and young adults are still developing the skills to navigate their life paths effectively. One might assume that technology would make these kinds of tasks easier to accomplish, but they still require analysis, human judgment, and discernment, strengths that young people are still developing.

There are no clear or consistent road maps for all young people to help them figure out what to do with their lives or how to approach getting it done. How exactly does an adolescent assess their own skills to determine what role might make the best first job? How do young people find training programs that match up with their interests? How does a young person know how to pivot if their initial plan is not a good fit? I liken it to the effort required to do your taxes, except instead of happening once a year, the need to "figure it out" continues for adolescents every day as they grow into adulthood. Yes, there might be instructions for preparing your taxes, but the work can be complicated and getting it wrong is costly and high stakes. And even if there is a free tax-prep program, how would you know it existed?

I believe going through adolescence is a similar experience for many young people. Many are navigating blindly among different services, resources, programs, and adult guidance as they move from high school to work, college, and careers. Some young people are also parents, trying to manage all of these things for themselves while also navigating systems and supports to take care of a child. For these young parents and youth who are in foster care, involved in the juvenile justice system, or living in low-income households, the pressure is on to get these things right as much as possible because these young people have little wiggle room to absorb a misstep or an errant effort that takes them off track.

Collaborating to Ensure Adolescents Thrive by 25

Each of the sectors I have described in the previous chapters in this section—public systems, education, business, and the social sector—offer something unique in serving adolescents. Each of the Thrive by 25 areas—basic needs, permanent connections, education and credentials, financial stability, and youth leadership—are interdependent and build on each other, and they cannot be effectively addressed in isolation. The challenges adolescents face today are complex, so figuring out how these various entities can collaborate to deliver (rather than require young people to assemble) the right set of supports at the right time is essential.

When they do, they can create a more holistic and supportive environment for adolescents on their journey to adulthood. When these systems integrate and collaborate, they can create not just a "safety net" that addresses immediate concerns, but also an "opportunity trampoline" that empowers and propels young people toward adulthood with confidence and resilience.

I know what you might be thinking as I describe this. Perhaps something along the lines of this: "But there is growth that comes from self-agency! Young people need to go through these experiences as part of growing up—I did and I made it through."

I agree—especially as the parent of a young person in college. But the normal life challenges that our young people face need to be at the scale that they can manage successfully. It does no one, including society, any good if our young people's futures are left up to chance, if they have to figure this out on their own without the benefit of strong guidance. We as adults have to take responsibility for the coordination and navigation that our young people need.

Children's Cabinets

Responsibility can take several forms. "Children's cabinets" housed within government represent one formal structure that system leaders have put into practice to align their decision-making on behalf of young people.[1] Typically these are a kind of interagency coordinating body—sometimes within a governor's office or a city or state agency—that is made up of representatives of departments and agencies that serve children, like education, human services, child welfare, juvenile justice, and child care.[2]

By including experts from all sectors that impact children's lives, children's cabinets help ensure that policies are informed by a comprehensive range of perspectives. This collective wisdom can lead to more well-rounded and effective policies, as it considers the diverse needs of children from different angles. Also, children's cabinets can help create a shared vision across agencies and with external nonprofits and other partners to increase public awareness on youth issues.[3]

For example, Indiana has a very structured approach through its Commission on Improving the Status of Children. One of the tools it created was a state agency program map.[4] This all-in-one-place resource shows an interactive list of Indiana's child-serving agencies' programs by age range served, and it connects to more information about specific eligibility requirements. Imagine how useful this is to the government, nonprofits, and families as they work to ensure adolescents have what they need. And the effort to put something like this together—the meetings and conversations, as well as verifying and discovering—leads to new opportunities for collaboration and coordination.

Integrated Data Systems
Another way to collaborate is to connect the data from across the government or the nonprofit sector so that there is a more comprehensive view of a young person's strengths, needs, and existing support. This is one way that young people and their families who are seeking support across different systems can have more seamless experiences, and government actors and policymakers can make more effective decisions about allocating their resources.

In our work, I've seen systems, especially public ones, struggle with data integration. Think of a data sharing agreement that, within privacy guidelines, allows a juvenile court judge to read an adolescent's foster case file with a few taps on a screen. That kind of access is nearly impossible today because data are captured in different systems and are typically gathered for reporting purposes, not decision-making.

One issue that is common across systems is that decisions made in one area can affect another area negatively. And yet, competing policies could easily be avoided when there is a holistic look at data across systems. Washington state addressed this challenge when faced with budget pressure and a proposal to eliminate the practice to continue to pay out cash benefits (commonly known as TANF) to families when the child was in foster care. Analysts found a correlation between families that retained TANF benefits or had them cut to the length of time a child remained in foster care. With the data among multiple agencies aligned, officials were able to look at client records over time and see that more children whose parents kept their TANF benefits were reunited without much more cost to the state.[5] Since the cost of keeping the program was not dramatically different than cutting it, with those reunification results, the cash benefits continued to be paid out to families when their child went into foster care. This made it more likely the parents could meet their family's basic needs and create a stable environment for the child to return to. Policy officials could see the benefit of making decisions with combined data. David Stillman, assistant secretary of the Economic Services Administration, said: "Looking across systems allows us to take action so policies are not in conflict."

It is a major barrier for systems to have outdated technology. For example, in Texas, when a child is removed from their home and placed into foster care, their data go through ninety subprocess steps from nineteen distinct data sources.[6] Surely, this can and should be streamlined. Business has much better tools, which enables them to manage for much better outcomes.

To be sure, there are challenges that make it difficult for these kinds of data sharing arrangements to get off the ground, namely, very vital questions around privacy issues, determining governance and access rules, and negotiating and finalizing data sharing agreements. Then there is the public perspective of wanting to keep officials who have access to these data accountable for proper usage. But the benefits and improved efficiency as highlighted in these examples outweighs those challenges.

Service Integration

Another barrier to the systems working more cohesively is that they often provide separate services that could easily be combined. As an example, a parent has to visit one place for assistance with their child and then a different agency for their own help.

One approach is to integrate services so that families can be served holistically in one place, which is especially helpful for low-income families that may be trying to navigate public transportation. That means, for example, a health center that can see babies and parents on the same visit. Some institutions are moving in this direction—like when schools provide take-home meals, eliminating one item on a parent's to-do list and supporting a family with basic needs. There are even overhead savings opportunities when multiple health and human services agencies are located in the same physical space and can share equipment or staff, and broker partnerships between providers.[7] Using a model that is responsive to the a family's multiple needs would foster coordinated care, simplify referrals, improve service access, and boost communication.

The Casey Foundation has a long history of demonstrating the effectiveness of integrated services through a one-stop shop framework we developed called the Center for Working Families. The idea was to give people a central place to receive what we determined to be three core services related to their economic stability: employment services, help with accessing benefits, and financial literacy education.[8]

While initially developed to serve a range of adults, we worked to refine the Center for Working Families model to specifically support students in college. It was piloted with young people attending Central New Mexico Community College. Called CNM Connect, the program featured coaching that helped students set goals and assist them in applying to scholarships and completing their financial aid forms, which officials used as a way to talk to students about budgeting the financial awards they were hoping to receive. Studies of the CNM Connect program showed that participants realized important gains, including improvements in their credit scores.[9]

Another related issue is that families that need help encounter programs that have different eligibility requirements but require submission of the same information multiple times. One way to address this is through technology programs that consider a family's eligibility for multiple programs at one time, called an integrated eligibility system. Some of the features of these systems include people being able to apply for benefits through online eligibility interviews or completing applications by telephone, which supports individuals with limited mobility or unreliable transportation. That is a sharp contrast with the typical service model of an applicant needing to visit an office in person to complete hardcopy forms on their own and mail them. These types of small changes, along with technology improvements, show that it is possible to have a people-first perspective even with large complex systems.

Navigation

When something is new, confusing, or hard to accomplish alone, you need a guide. When I crossed the Arouca 516 bridge, I didn't do it alone. I had a guide who had traveled the path before and could give me tips for the journey. I still had to put one foot in front of the other and take my steps. It was scary but knowing that a guide was there reassured me to do so.

While the recommendations above around improving agency coordination, consolidating service locations, and integrating eligibility systems could make a big difference, the current reality is that young people still practicing and strengthening their executive functioning will need help to weave together everything from these multiple sectors. There are many processes and systems that young people interact with, and they can be complicated. Adolescents sure could use a guide.

Some systems they encounter may have support built in, but the experience is fragmented. For example, a young person may receive excellent feedback from a school guidance counselor about postsecondary opportunities, but that support does not include assistance with accessing health care because that topic is outside of their area of expertise. Different systems have different sources of data and terminology and often don't speak to each other. To get support, a young person has to learn and understand different rules, languages, protocols, and dynamics for what they want to accomplish—across fragmented systems.

The concept of having a navigator is growing in the social services field. A navigator could help young parents find childcare and connect to employment services while also referring them to programs for housing and other benefits.[10]

Navigation is important because of the specific tasks young people need to complete that are essential for their future. As I described in the chapter about employers, young people can take part in programs that reinforce their education and give them exposure to the workplace. But they need reliable information about skills and how to develop those skills through the opportunities that are available to them. This is especially true in communities with limited career pathways, which may not reflect the breadth of career interests of young people.

What youth and young adults need is navigation support that is centered around them as an individual, not the system. This support would go across systems to help young people create independent, thriving adult lives.

Aligning Efforts Across Systems

It would have been easy for officials in Washington state to react to the budget pressure by moving to cut the cash benefits for children out of the home—a move that would have introduced new hardships for hundreds of families. There is a cost to operating from a reactive stance, and it can be sizable. By contrast, a proactive approach calls for bringing systems together so their work is aligned and can deliver results on behalf of adolescents.

But how?

A different outcome requires doing something different, to approach solving issues as a collective rather than an individual or individual organization. Along with a group approach, it takes effective executive leadership to underpin the effort and steer it in a forward direction.

At Casey, we understand this approach and use it through the release of our annual *KIDS COUNT®* Data Book. Since 1990, Casey has published a national data book on children. The goal was to provide comprehensive data on child well-being to inform policymakers and encourage positive change.

KIDS COUNT has since grown into a powerful network and brand, with a presence across all fifty states and U.S. territories. One key lever to this expansion was inviting state-based child advocacy organizations to form a KIDS COUNT network and funding them to create cross-sector coalitions, helping them advance legislation on behalf of children, adolescents, and families, and equipping them to share the importance of this work with local stakeholders. When we reflect on the value of the KIDS COUNT initiative over more than 35 years, we can count policy victories in every state, and billions of dollars in new or protected investments, helping nearly all of the 74 million kids in this country in some way.[11] This speaks to what is possible when there's better connection in the ecosystem.

Around the country, this kind of collaborative effort is happening in new ways. One example is an initiative called Strive Together. The idea is to bring leadership across a community together with the goal of working together to address economic mobility by solving specific local barriers they identify.[12]

It is best to understand this approach in action. Baltimore recognized there were an alarming number of young people ages fourteen to twenty-four who were not in school or working. To solve this problem, Baltimore's Promise (the local StriveTogether network member), the Mayor's Office of Employment Development, and Baltimore City Public Schools have collaborated to create Grads2Careers (G2C). The program offers skills training, mentorship, and internship opportunities to high school graduates. It is all about connecting young people in Baltimore to career and postsecondary opportunities.

The program helps high school grads gain immediate skills training to improve their job prospects. In the first phase, 400 participants completed training, 257 found jobs, and 35 enrolled in college, resulting in a 76 percent success rate.[13] What's even more impressive is that G2C grads, especially African American males and females, are earning significantly more than their peers from the class of 2009—22 percent more for men and 33 percent more for women. This initiative is a great example of how targeted support can really make a difference in both careers and future earnings.

Government, the social sector, business, and education are each large systems in their own right, working to serve constituents and clients and deliver results. On behalf of adolescents, what is needed is for those sectors to start, and to continue, to collaborate to create new and improved outcomes. We need today's young people to become tomorrow's elected officials, nonprofit leaders, business executives, and educators. They benefit when different sectors can come together purposefully on their behalf to coordinate efforts and create improved outcomes—and better lives—for all children, youth, and young adults.

Conclusion

My journey across the Arouca 516 bridge in Portugal ended when I made it to the other side. But the experience left me curious about the inspiration for the bridge design—the ancient rope bridges built by hand by the Incas. So, I looked up the history.

The Incas built bridges by collecting strands of local *ichu* grass, carefully twisting the hay-colored strands into ropes, and braiding the larger ropes together to make long, heavy cables. Then the villagers would carry the cables to a canyon to stretch and knot them as part of the construction and installation of a bridge.[1]

This way of building bridges has continued for hundreds of years and is still practiced today. In one Peruvian town in the Andes Mountains, the entire village comes together once a year to replace the last remaining rope bridge as a form of community service. Once complete, they celebrate with a ceremony that includes food, music, and prayer.[2] This community effort to maintain the bridge involves everyone.

What a perfect metaphor for the bridge we in the United States need to build and maintain today for adolescents so that they have safe passage to adulthood. We can take our individual efforts and weave them together until they are strong and reliable—not working for individual gain but for the betterment of all. Like the Inca bridges that inspired Arouca, the people, communities, and institutions that surround young people must invest in a strong bridge through adolescence like any critical infrastructure, supporting each young person as they take steps forward. Their successful passage into adulthood means a stronger society for all of us.

Conclusion

Whether it is the government stewarding and protecting young people and their families through the public services they provide, or an employer providing an apprenticeship opportunity, or nonprofits mentoring and engaging young people to shape their unfolding lives, all of us have a role to play in ensuring safe passage for young people. We must fundamentally shift policies, practices, and systems to not only address the challenges adolescents face, but also prioritize their success. Let's build a bridge that all young people can successfully traverse—not one that's less difficult for some. That is the only way to ensure the future of our families, communities, businesses, and country.

Every adult was once an adolescent.

Just like we once did, each young person today must walk across their individual bridge to adulthood—at times feeling confident, at other times feeling nervous and making mistakes along the way. But they can't make it all the way across if the deck of the bridge is missing or damaged or there is no guidance to instruct them where to walk. That's our role. Now more than ever, we must provide the structure and support young people need to safely navigate these transitions and build stable, fulfilling lives.

I imagine some adults are reflecting on their teenage journeys thinking, *"Well I survived. Why can't they? Why does it seem like young people today need so much more help?"* That is a fair question. But as I was raising my daughter, who is now in her twenties, I saw firsthand how her life is quite different from mine. Young people today face a set of challenges far different from what earlier generations encountered.

Technological Pressures

Technology is hailed as a great equalizer and productivity tool, but its implications on the lives of young people are complex. When I was an adolescent, I wasn't expected to keep track of my homework assignments and grades via digital learning platforms. I didn't have to apply to jobs online and hope that my application wasn't weeded out by an algorithm. I didn't have a constant stream of perfect images from Instagram coming at me when I was eleven, and you probably didn't either. It's no wonder that the rapid rise of technology and its near saturation in our daily lives is stressful for adolescents.

Economic Uncertainty

Young people today are also facing high levels of economic uncertainty—not just navigating the ups and downs of the stock market, but seismic shifts in the pathways into work, types of jobs available, and the compensation and benefits that are offered. It's estimated that by 2031, the share of well-paying jobs that require some postsecondary education will jump to 66 percent, a number that's increased over time.[3] The average price of college is also increasing,[4] putting an education out of reach for many, particularly low-income and first-generation aspiring college students. The prevalence of freelance work and gig work through social media apps is also dramatically reshaping the economy. It enables millions of people to earn money with flexibility but without benefits like workplace-provided health insurance or retirement benefits. Young people are increasingly uncertain about their future careers and financial stability.

Social Fragmentation

In 2023, the U.S. Surgeon General launched an effort to bring attention to what he called the country's growing epidemic of loneliness and isolation. Social connection—the structure, function, and quality of our relationships with others—is a critical and underappreciated contributor to individual and population health, community safety, resilience, and prosperity.[5] Our relationships and interactions with family, friends, colleagues, and neighbors are just some of what create social connection. Our connection with others and our community is also informed by our neighborhoods, digital environments, schools, and workplaces.

With more activity happening online and fewer social institutions to bring people together, young adults are almost twice as likely to report feeling lonely than those older than sixty-five. The rate of loneliness among young adults has increased every year between 1976 and 2019. This means young people today on average have fewer relationships to draw upon for encouragement and support.

Global Challenges

And if these differences aren't enough, young people must also confront a societal and political context that includes issues like climate change, social justice movements, political instability, and incivility. That leaves many young people today feeling like they have little control over their future, and that the system is unfairly rigged against them.[6] It's particularly disheartening when the brain science of this stage of life is primed for exploring new possibilities and dreaming of a better future.

This is a lot for young people to process or feel confident that they can successfully navigate. These dynamic changes are upending typical and established societal guideposts and guardrails. As a result, the path forward for youth has become more complex and uncertain. Their lives are not like ours. That's why the infrastructure that existed for us no longer works for them. If we want the next generation to succeed, we must reflect on what they need now and create environments that truly support their growth and well-being.[7]

A possible antidote to this array of issues is more face-to-face connection. More community and positive social interactions can make teens and young people feel like they belong to something bigger than themselves. In-person relationships can help them navigate the maze of online life so that their talents and potential can be considered, by themselves and by others. They need tangible economic support that is easy to access and tailor made for their time of life. Plus, clear information and pathways to the education and careers that will propel them forward. All of these things help give our young people safe passage across the bridge to adulthood.

While we as adults continue to live our lives and chart our future, our young people are right there alongside us. They need to receive reassurance and to be taught resilience in the face of so many large unknowns.

Because isn't that what we want our young people to learn in this in-between time in their lives—how to move forward despite not knowing the exact way? We want them to persist, to build life skills, to grow in confidence, and to learn from mistakes. We want our young people to discover what they want and what they don't want for their lives.

Human adolescence is the longest of any species because it takes time and experience to make it across that bridge. The process is meant to connect us to the best parts of ourselves and unleash our potential. That is the most joyous feeling, to know that you are capable and strong and have agency over your life. Shouldn't we want all young people to experience this so they can become who they are meant to be?

When adolescents do cross the bridge, their journey isn't over. Their adult lives are just beginning. And if we've done our jobs well, young people go forward with all that they've learned on the crossing. With the people who supported them. With the stability a bright future requires. And with the knowledge that they can be leaders in their own lives and in the world they help to build. That is what it means for them to thrive.

Acknowledgments

Writing a book is something I never thought I would do, but when I met Adriana Galván of the UCLA Center for the Developing Adolescent and heard her describe the promise and potential of the adolescent brain, I knew I had stumbled onto someone and something special. She was the first person to introduce me to the field of adolescent brain science, and she translated the science in such an accessible way that it was eye opening and inspiring to know that we had another tool at our disposal to get better outcomes for young people. In many ways, this book and the innovations we have been able to lead at the Casey Foundation based on adolescent brain science would not have happened without Galván and the team at the center. Thank you for your tireless, groundbreaking research and for patiently sharing it with the world.

In the early days of book research, Andrew Reinel, Beatriz Lopes, Amnoni Myers, and Aby Washington were so generous with their time and insights.

I enjoy writing, but this book was a challenge that exceeded my available time and expertise. I am eternally grateful to my creative collaborator and writing guide Theola DeBose for her extraordinary contributions and partnership in bringing this book to life. Theola consumed thousands of pages of research, reports, and blogs and conducted countless interviews to immerse herself in the science of adolescence and our work. She also spent innumerable hours just talking to me, pulling out the stories of my life and my perspective so that she could capture my views and voice. As we

Acknowledgments

neared the end of this project, she texted me to say how honored she was that I trusted her with my voice. In reality, she helped me find mine.

To Marc Favreau and the entire team at The New Press, you got the concept of this book right away and your belief in the project was the undercurrent that kept us moving forward especially when it got hard. Thank you for getting us over the finish line. I am so happy to be publishing with you.

I am grateful for the essential support of the board of trustees of the Annie E. Casey Foundation when I decided to make adolescence central to our organizational strategy and launched Thrive By 25. I hope that you remain proud of the important contributions we are making to improve practice, policy, and programs for young people during this critical and often misunderstood stage of life.

I am grateful to every colleague at the Annie E. Casey Foundation (past and present) whose hard work, innovation, and experience shaped this book. I particularly want to thank the Foundation's portfolio directors, whose genius powers our accomplishments.

To the vice presidents—Leslie Boissiere, Sandra Gasca, Allison Gerber, Thomasina Hiers, Stephen Plank, John Kim, Katie Tetrault, Kimberley Brown, Xander Perry, and Patrice Cromwell who left this life too soon—you are individually and collectively the definition of leadership. You read every word and your thoughtful feedback is on every page. Your partnership has been a blessing to me every single day.

Kelley Acree, Pat McMahon, and Stanley Fontaine: Thank you for your unwavering support and for always making sure I have what I need and get where I need to go.

Kate Shatzkin, Norris West, and Arin Gencer, your big idea is now a reality. Thanks for launching us on this journey and for your hard work to keep us on track.

Laura Speer, I am enriched every day as you share the breadth

Acknowledgments

of your knowledge and appreciate all the ways you brought your institutional memory, ideas, and aspirations for our work to inform this book.

Alexandra West, you are the best project and people manager I know. You managed this book with so much grace and determination. I can't thank you enough for every problem you solved, every wise suggestion you made, every time you succinctly synthesized mountains of feedback, and every ounce of faith you put in me that this book would happen. I don't know how you do it, but I am grateful that you do.

I offer special appreciation to my predecessors as president of the Annie E. Casey Foundation, Doug Nelson and Patrick McCarthy, who have been inspirations, friends, and confidants in my own journey as a leader.

My parents George and Jacquelyn Lawson guided me on my bridge from adolescence to adulthood with love, support, and opportunities. Your respect for me and openness with me during that uncertain time in my life set the foundation for every success I have experienced as an adult. I am so blessed to have my mother's continued support beside me in this life, and I know my father is looking down from heaven beaming with pride.

To my life partner, Cheis Garrus, we met and found love as adolescents during our first years of college. How lucky are we that we get to continue our story decades later. Thank you for seeing me, loving me, believing in me, and always caring for me in the most thoughtful ways.

Finally, to Lauren Hamilton, my daughter and single biggest inspiration for learning more about adolescence. You have a few years before your adolescence is officially over, but I couldn't be more proud or more in awe of the ways you have navigated this time in your life. I've watched you propel yourself—sometimes crawling and sometimes leaping—toward the person you want and are meant to be. Thank you for letting me share a window into your life journey with those who read this book. Thank you for trusting me with your fears and dreams. Thank you for letting me bear witness to your metamorphosis into an amazing young woman. Thank you for being patient with me as your mom praying every day that I do the right things so you can thrive. We're coming through this experience not just as family, but as friends. I love you with all my heart.

Notes

Chapter 1: The Adolescent Brain

1. "516 Arouca," 516 Arouca, accessed December 16, 2024.

2. National Academies of Sciences, Engineering, and Medicine. *The Promise of Adolescence: Realizing Opportunity for All Youth*. (Washington, D.C.: The National Academies Press, 2019.)

3. Samuels, Lisa. "How Big Is the Brain?" *Verywell Mind*, November 6, 2023.

4. Samuels, Lisa. "Synapse Anatomy," *Verywell Health*, November 6, 2023.

5. Siegel, Daniel J., and Tina Payne Bryson. *The Whole-Brain Child*. (New York: Delacorte Press, 2011.)

6. Miles, Karen. "The Terrible Twos Are Very Real: Here's How to Cope," BabyCenter, March 6, 2024.

7. "Anatomy of the Brain," Johns Hopkins Medicine, accessed December 1, 2024.

8. "What Is Executive Function and How Does It Relate to Child Development?" Harvard University Center on the Developing Child, accessed December 1, 2024.

9. Winters, K.C., and A. Arria. "Adolescent Brain Development and Drugs," *Prevention Research* 18, no. 2 (2011): 21–24.

10. Galván, Adriana. "The Teenage Brain: Sensitivity to Rewards," *Current Directions in Psychological Science* 22, no. 2 (2013): 88–93.

11. Maldarelli, Claire. "Humans Are the Only Animals to Go Through Teenage Rebellion, but a Few Species Come Close," *Popular Science*, May 8, 2018.

12. Rosati, Alexandra G., et al. "Distinct Developmental Trajectories for Risky and Impulsive Decision-Making in Chimpanzees," *Journal of Experimental Psychology: General*, American Psychological Association, 2023.

13. Adriana Galván, conversation with the author, April 3, 2023.

Chapter 2: Challenges Adolescents Face

1. Peverill, Matthew, Maya L. Rosen, Lucy A. Lurie, Kelly A. Sambrook, Margaret A. Sheridan, and Katie A. McLaughlin. "Childhood Trauma and Brain Structure in Children and Adolescents," *Developmental Cognitive Neuroscience* 59 (2023): 101–80.

2. Ibid.

3. "Neuroplasticity," *Psychology Today*, accessed December 1, 2024.

4. "Adverse Childhood Experiences (ACEs)," CPTSD Foundation, October 7, 2019.

5. Felitti, Vincent J. "The Relation Between Adverse Childhood Experiences and Adult Health: Turning Gold into Lead," *The Permanente Journal* 6, no. 1 (Winter 2002): 44–47.

6. Felitti, Vincent J., Robert F. Anda, Dale Nordenberg, David F. Williamson, Alison M. Spitz, Valerie Edwards, Mary P. Koss, and James S. Marks. "Relationship of Childhood Abuse and Household Dysfunction to Many of the Leading Causes of Death in Adults: The Adverse Childhood Experiences (ACE) Study," *American Journal of Preventive Medicine* 14, no. 4 (1998): 245–58.

7. "Adverse Childhood Experiences (ACEs)," Centers for Disease Control and Prevention, modified November 28, 2024.

8. "Prevalence of Adverse Childhood Experiences Nationally, by State, and by Race/Ethnicity," Child Trends, modified November 28, 2024.

9. Crouch, E., E. Radcliff, M. Strompolis, and A. Srivastav. "Safe, Stable, and Nurtured: Protective Factors Against Poor Physical and Mental Health Outcomes Following Exposure to Adverse Childhood Experiences (ACEs)," *Journal of Child & Adolescent Trauma* 12, no. 2 (2018): 165–73.

10. Bellis, Mark A., Karen Hughes, Kat Ford, Katie A. Hardcastle, Catherine A. Sharp, Sara Wood, Lucia Homolova, and Alisha Davies. "Does Continuous Trusted Adult Support in Childhood Impart Life-Course Resilience Against Adverse Childhood Experiences: A Retrospective Study on Adult Health-Harming Behaviours and Mental Well-Being," *BMC Psychiatry* 17, no. 1 (2017): 110.

11. Balistreri, Kelly S., and Martha Alvira-Hammond. "Adverse Childhood Experiences, Family Functioning and Adolescent Health and Emotional Well-Being," *Public Health* 132 (March 2016): 72–78.

12. "Toxic Stress," Center on the Developing Child at Harvard University, accessed November 28, 2024.

13. "About Child Trauma," National Child Traumatic Stress Network, accessed November 28, 2024.

14. "ACEs and Toxic Stress: Frequently Asked Questions," Center on the Developing Child at Harvard University, accessed November 28, 2024.

15. "How Poverty in the United States Is Measured and Why It Matters," Population Reference Bureau, modified November 28, 2024.

16. "No Place for Kids: The Case for Reducing Juvenile Incarceration," The Annie E. Casey Foundation, October 4, 2011.

17. "Don't Abandon Us: Addressing Youth Crime and Trauma," Justice Policy Institute, YouTube, September 2023.

18. Powers, Makia E., Jennifer Takagishi, et al. "Care of Adolescent Parents and Their Children," *Pediatrics* 147, no. 5 (May 2021): e2021050919.

19. "The AFCARS Report: Preliminary FY 2021 Estimates as of October 2022, No. 30," Administration for Children and Families, Children's Bureau, Washington, DC: U.S. Department of Health and Human Services, 2022.

20. Hessing, Abigail. "Sexual Abuse of Children in the United States Foster Care System," Ballard Brief, accessed December 16, 2024.

Chapter 3: A New Approach

1. Saxon, Wolfgang. "James E. Casey Is Dead at 95; Started United Parcel Service," *The New York Times*, June 7, 1983.

2. Internal, unpublished corporate history of the United Parcel Service.

3. Ibid.

4. "Thrive by 25: Casey Foundation Announces Increased Focus on Youth and Young Adults," The Annie E. Casey Foundation, modified August 12, 2021.

5. "Children in Poverty," The Annie E. Casey Foundation KIDS COUNT Data Center, accessed November 28, 2024.

Chapter 4: Basic Needs

1. Cherry, Kendra. "What Is Maslow's Hierarchy of Needs?" *Verywell Mind*, modified September 14, 2023.

2. Copley, Laura. "Hierarchy of Needs: A 2024 Take on Maslow's Findings," *Positive Psychology*, modified February 24, 2024.

3. "Key Statistics & Graphics," U.S. Department of Agriculture, Economic Research Service, modified November 2024.

4. Goldrick-Rab, Sara, Christine Baker-Smith, Vanessa Coca, Elizabeth Looker, and Tiffani Williams. *College and University Basic Needs Insecurity: A National #RealCollege Survey Report*, The Hope Center for College, Community, and Justice, April 2019.

5. "Youth Homelessness Overview," National Conference of State Legislatures, modified November 2024.

Notes

6. Cutuli, Jennifer J., Kristin L. Wiik, Jessica E. Herbers, Megan R. Gunnar, and Ann S. Masten. "Cortisol Function Among Early School-Aged Homeless Children," *Psychoneuroendocrinology* 35, no. 6 (July 2010): 833–45.

7. "The Education of Children and Youth Experiencing Homelessness: Current Trends, Challenges, and Needs," SchoolHouse Connection, modified November 2024.

8. Duncan, Greg J., Jennifer Appleton Gootman, and Priyanka Nalamada, editors. *Reducing Intergenerational Poverty*, National Academies of Sciences, Engineering, and Medicine (Washington, D.C.: *The National Academies Press*, 2024).

9. Fowler, Paul J., David B. Henry, and Katherine E. Marcal. "Family and Housing Instability: Longitudinal Impact on Adolescent Emotional and Behavioral Well-Being," *Social Science Research* 53 (2015): 364–74.

10. "Two-Bedroom Housing Wage in the U.S. by State," Statista, modified November 2024.

11. *Adolescent Health: A Research Brief*, Kaiser Permanente, 2024.

12. "Children's Mental Health Data," Centers for Disease Control and Prevention, modified November 2024.

13. Steinberg, Laurence. "A Social Neuroscience Perspective on Adolescent Risk-Taking," *Developmental Review* 28, no. 1 (2008): 78–106. The influence of peers in adolescence comes from the fact that adolescents spend more time in peer groups, and researchers believe that just by being in each other's company this activates the same parts of the adolescent's brain that seeks rewards.

14. "Children Are Dying at the Highest Rate in 13 Years," USA Facts, modified 2023.

15. Sokol, Rebeccah L., Maya Haasz, Marc A. Zimmerman, Rebecca M. Cunningham, and Patrick M. Carter. "The Association Between Witnessing Firearm Violence and Firearm Carriage: Results from a National Study of Teens," *Preventive Medicine* 171 (2023): 107516.

16. "What's the Big Data?" Smartphone Stats, accessed December 1, 2024.

17. "FCC Broadband Overreporting by State," BroadbandNow, modified September 2023.

18. "Teens, Social Media and Technology 2022," Pew Research Center, modified August 10, 2022.

19. "Frequently Asked Questions Related to the Poverty Guidelines," U.S. Department of Health and Human Services, accessed December 1, 2024.

20. *Income and Poverty in the United States: 2020*, U.S. Census Bureau, accessed 2021.

21. "America's Diverse Adolescents," U.S. Department of Health and Human Services, Office of Population Affairs, accessed December 1, 2024.

22. "Overview," United for ALICE, modified 2024.

23. "National Overview," United for ALICE, modified 2024.

24. "Focus on Children," United for ALICE, modified 2024.

25. Radeva, Aleksandra, Lisa Simon, and James Enright. "More Than 36% of Russell 1000 Workers Don't Make a Family-Sustaining Living Wage," JUST Capital, March 12, 2024.

26. *Federal Social Safety Net Programs: Millions of Full-Time Workers Rely on Federal Health Care and Food Assistance Programs,* GAO-21-45, Washington, D.C., U.S. Government Accountability Office, October 19, 2020.

27. Noble, Kimberly G., Katherine Magnuson, Lisa A. Gennetian, Greg J. Duncan, Hirokazu Yoshikawa, Nathan A. Fox, and Sarah Halpern-Meekin. "Baby's First Years: Design of a Randomized Controlled Trial of Poverty Reduction in the United States," *Pediatrics* 148, no. 4 (October 2021): e2020049702.

Chapter 5: Permanent Connections

1. Cancel, Sixto. "Innovating the American Foster Care System," TED Talks, November 2018, accessed December 15, 2024.

2. U.S. Department of Health and Human Services, Administration for Children and Families, Children's Bureau, Adoption and Foster Care Analysis and Reporting System (AFCARS) Report No. 29, 2022.

3. Ibid.

4. Stoltzfus, Emilie. *Child Welfare: Purposes, Federal Programs, and Funding,* Congressional Research Service, updated October 1, 2024.

5. For this analysis, 2021 AFCARS categories of "child behavior," "child alcohol use," and "child drug abuse" are combined. Note that AFCARS categories for removal reasons are not mutually exclusive, so a removal may be counted in more than one category. U.S. Department of Health and Human Services, AFCARS Report, 2022.

6. Benzi, Ilaria Maria Antonietta, Nicola Carone, Marlene Moretti, Laura Ruglioni, Jacopo Tracchegiani, and Lavinia Barone. "eCONNECT Parent Group: An Online Attachment-Based Intervention to Reduce Attachment Insecurity, Behavioral Problems, and Emotional Dysregulation in Adolescence," *International Journal of Environmental Research and Public Health* 20, no. 4 (2023): 3532.

7. "SOUL Family Permanency Option," The Annie E. Casey Foundation, November 19, 2024.

8. "Human Trafficking and Child Welfare: A Guide for Child Welfare Agencies," U.S. Department of Health and Human Services, Administration for Children and Families, Child Welfare Information Gateway, Children's Bureau, 2023.

9. Amani, Bita, Norweeta G. Milburn, Susana Lopez, Angela Young-Brinn, Lourdes Castro, Alex Lee, and Eraka Bath. "Families and the Juvenile Justice

System: Considerations for Family-Based Interventions," *Family & Community Health* 41, no. 1 (January/March 2018): 55–63.

10. "Delinquency Cases in 2019," U.S. Department of Justice, Office of Justice Programs, 2020.

11. *"Juvenile Court Statistics 2019,"* U.S. Department of Justice, Office of Justice Programs, 2021.

12. *A Guide for Families and Professionals,* Office of Juvenile Justice and Delinquency Prevention, 2021.

13. Goldstein, Naomi E.S., et al. " 'You're on the Right Track!' Using Graduated Response Systems to Address Immaturity of Judgment and Enhance Youths' Capacities to Successfully Complete Probation," *Temple Law Review* 88 (2016): 803–836.

14. "Pierce County: Trailblazer for Probation Transformation," The Annie E. Casey Foundation, May 28, 2018.

15. "Incentives Inspire Positive Behavior Change in Youth on Probation," The Annie E. Casey Foundation, March 30, 2020.

16. Ibid.

17. "Who Mentored You? A Study Examining the Role Mentors Have Played in the Lives of Americans over the Last Half Century," Mentoring.org, 2023.

18. "What We Do," Thread, accessed December 2024.

Chapter 6: Education and Credentials

1. "Meet the 2023 Washingtonians of the Year," *Washingtonian,* January 8, 2024.

2. "Nicole Lynn Lewis on Helping Young Student Parents and Their Kids Excel," The Annie E. Casey Foundation, January 8, 2024.

3. "Meet the 2023 Washingtonians of the Year," *Washingtonian.*

4. "College Enrollment and Work Activity of High School Graduates News Release," U.S. Bureau of Labor Statistics, April 23, 2024.

5. Zimmerman, E., and S. H. Woolf. "Understanding the Relationship Between Education and Health," NAM Perspectives, Discussion Paper, National Academy of Medicine, Washington, DC, 2014.

6. "Report on the Condition of Education, High School Graduation Rates," U.S. Department of Education, Institute of Education Sciences, accessed December 2024.

7. Ibid.

8. "Non-Regulatory Guidance: Ensuring Educational Stability for Children in Foster Care," U.S. Department of Education, accessed December 2024.

9. "High School Alternatives Scan: A Report on High School Alternative Programs in the Northwest," Education Northwest, accessed December 15, 2024.

10. Ibid.

11. "What Teens Want from Their Schools," Fordham Institute, accessed December 15, 2024.

12. "High School Diploma Gives David Ramirez a Fresh Start," Goodwill Indy Blog, accessed December 15, 2024.

13. "Current Term Enrollment Estimates: Fall 2024," National Student Clearinghouse Research Center, accessed February 5, 2025.

14. "High School Benchmarks," National Student Clearinghouse Research Center, accessed December 15, 2024.

15. Hanson, Melanie. "Student Loan Debt by Race," EducationData.org, May 13, 2024.

Chapter 7: Financial Stability and Well-Being

1. "Meet Our Alumni: Esther Aidelomon, IT Support," by Per Scholas, YouTube, posted December 14, 2022.

2. Ashburn, Elyse. "A Much-Watched Tech Program Aims to Give Alumni a Second Bite at a 'Good Job,' " *Workshift*, September 21, 2023.

3. "50 Ways the Workforce Has Changed in 50 Years," *Stacker*, November 9, 2023.

4. Ibid.

5. "Youth Employment and Unemployment—December 2023," news release, U.S. Bureau of Labor Statistics, January 5, 2024.

6. Irwin, V., et al. *Report on the Condition of Education 2024*, National Center for Education Statistics, 2024.

7. Mortimer, Jeylan T. "The Benefits and Risks of Adolescent Employment," *Preventive Research* 17, no. 2 (2010): 8–11.

8. "The Future of Jobs Report 2023," World Economic Forum, 2023.

9. *Apprenticeships: The Ticket to Our Future*, Young Invincibles, 2024.

10. "Apprentice: Beyond Construction," U.S. Bureau of Labor Statistics, Career Outlook, 2022.

11. "Promises of Summer Youth Employment Programs: Lessons from Randomized Evaluations," The Abdul Latif Jameel Poverty Action Lab, accessed December 15, 2024.

12. Heller, Sara, Harold Pollack, and Jonathan M.V. Davis. "Final Technical Report for Grant 2012-MU-FX-0002: The Effects of Summer Jobs on Youth Violence," August 2017.

13. "Seasonally Adjusted Monthly Youth Unemployment Rate in the U.S.," Statista, accessed December 15, 2024.

14. "Youth and Work: Restoring Teen and Young Adult Connections to Opportunity," The Annie E. Casey Foundation, March 1, 2012.

15. Bryan, J. "Why Wages Aren't Growing in America," *Harvard Business Review,* October 10, 2017, accessed December 15, 2024.

16. Ross, Martha, and Nicole Bateman. *Meet the Low-Wage Workforce*, Brookings, November 2019, accessed December 15, 2024.

17. Ibid.

Chapter 8: Youth Leadership: Taking Charge of Their Lives

1. "Naomi Wadler on Raising Youth Voices and Youth Advocates," The Annie E. Casey Foundation, accessed December 14, 2024.

2. Burack, Emily. "Activist Naomi Wadler Celebrates Her Bat Mitzvah," Kveller, accessed December 14, 2024.

3. Tackett, Jennifer L., Kathleen W. Reardon, Nathaniel J. Fast, Lynn Johnson, Sonia K. Kang, Jonas W. B. Lang, and Frederick L. Oswald. "Understanding the Leaders of Tomorrow: The Need to Study Leadership in Adolescence," *Perspectives on Psychological Science* 18, no. 4 (2023): 829–42.

4. "Achieving Authentic Youth Engagement: Core Values and Guiding Principles," The Annie E. Casey Foundation, 2000.

5. "A Framework for Effectively Partnering With Young People," The Annie E. Casey Foundation, 2019.

6. Garibaldi, Rosie. *LOUD Presentation*, Legislative Health and Human Services Committee, New Mexico Legislature, presented September 21, 2015, accessed December 14, 2024.

7. Desai, Shiv. "Formerly Incarcerated Teens Share Their Research Ideas to Improve the Juvenile Justice System," *The Current GA*, August 5, 2021, accessed December 14, 2024.

Chapter 9: The Ecosystem It Takes to Thrive

1. "National Parks," Visit Costa Rica, accessed March 9, 2024.

2. Definition of *ecosystem*, Biology Dictionary, accessed March 9, 2024.

3. "Head Start Founder Urie Bronfenbrenner Dies at 88," *Cornell Chronicle*, modified September 26, 2005.

4. "Ecosystems of Belonging: Reimagining Systems of Education and Care for Children," The Annie E. Casey Foundation, 2023.

5. "50 Years Later, Recalling the Founder of Head Start," *Cornell News*, May 28, 2015, accessed December 14, 2024.

6. "Bronfenbrenner's Ecological Systems Theory," *Simply Psychology*, modified 2024.

7. "Supportive Relationships and Active Skill-Building Strengthen the Foundations of Resilience: Working Paper 13," National Scientific Council on the Developing Child, 2015.

8. Moore, Kristin, Lina Guzman, Elizabeth Hair, Laura Lippman, and Sarah Garrett. "Parent-Teen Relationships and Interactions: Far More Positive Than Not," Child Trends in Research, 2004.

9. "Craving Opportunity: Baltimore Youth Describe What They Need for a Better Future," The Annie E. Casey Foundation, July 26, 2017.

10. *Creating Equitable Ecosystems of Belonging and Opportunity for Youth: An Action Guide for Cross-System and Sector Leaders and Practitioners*, The Forum for Youth Investment, March 2023.

11. Ibid.

12. Ibid.

Chapter 10: Public Systems and Policymakers

1. Moore, Wes. *The Other Wes Moore: One Name, Two Fates* (New York: Spiegel & Grau, 2010).

2. *Child Welfare Financing: Executive Summary*, Child Trend, May 2021.

3. "The Science Is Clear: Separating Families Has Long-Term Damaging Psychological and Health Consequences for Children, Families, and Communities," Society for Research in Child Development, June 20, 2018.

4. "Federal Foster Care Financing: How and Why the Current Funding Structure Fails to Meet the Needs of the Child Welfare Field," U.S. Department of Health and Human Services, 2021.

5. "Evidence to Impact: State Policy Options to Increase Access to Economic and Concrete Supports as a Child Welfare Prevention Strategy," American Public Human Services Association, Chapin Hall at the University of Chicago, June 2023.

6. "Who We Are," Thriving Families, Safer Children, accessed December 15, 2024.

7. Ibid.

8. Klika, J.B., et al. "Using the Core Components of a Public Health Framework to Create a Child and Family Well-being System: Example from a National Effort, Thriving Families, Safer Children," *International Journal of Child Maltreatment* 5, no. 4 (2022): 453–72.

9. "New Survey Aims to Improve Programs and Services for Youth in Memphis," Fox13 Memphis, updated July 25, 2023.

10. "System Reforms to Reduce Youth Incarceration: Why We Must Explore Every Option Before Removing Any Young Person from Home," The Sentencing Project, accessed December 15, 2024.

11. "Awards & Recognition," Alaska Native Medical Center, accessed December 15, 2024.

12. "Community-Driven Development at Pittsburgh Yards," The Annie E. Casey Foundation, accessed December 15, 2024.

13. "Support from Parents and Other Caring Adults," UCLA Center for the Developing Adolescent, accessed December 15, 2024.

14. "Family-Engaged Case Planning: Strengthening Partnerships with Families to Improve Outcomes for Children and Youth (2022)," The Annie E. Casey Foundation, accessed December 15, 2024.

15. Ibid.

16. "Team Decision Making (TDM)," The California Evidence-Based Clearinghouse for Child Welfare, February 2025, accessed April 7, 2025.

17. "How Many People are Served by the Social Safety Net? (2022)," U.S. Department of Health and Human Services, accessed December 15, 2024.

18. Ibid.

19. Canfield-Davis, Kathy, Sachin Jain, Donald K. Wattam, Jerry R. McMurtry, and M. Johnson. "Factors of Influence on Legislative Decision Making: A Descriptive Study Updated August 2009," *Journal of Legal, Ethical and Regulatory Issues* 13, no. 2 (2010): 55.

20. Ibid.

21. "Why Youth Incarceration Fails: An Updated Review of the Evidence," The Sentencing Project, March 1, 2023.

22. "Youth Master Plan," Minneapolis Youth Coordinating Board, 2019.

23. "Youth Master Plan Recommendations, 2020," City of Minneapolis Youth Coordinating Board, accessed December 15, 2024.

Chapter 11: Employers

1. Ross, Martha, Kristin Anderson Moore, Kelly Murphy, Nicole Bateman, Alex DeMand, and Vanessa Sacks. *Pathways to High-Quality Jobs for Young Adults*, Brookings Institution and Child Trends, October 2018, accessed December 15, 2024.

2. "The Teen Brain: 7 Things to Know," National Institute of Mental Health, accessed December 15, 2024.

Notes

3. "Hybrid Work," Gallup, accessed March 10, 2025.

4. "Impact of Technology on Young People: Shaping the Future Workforce," Build With Robots, accessed December 15, 2024.

5. "The Future of Jobs Report 2023," World Economic Forum, accessed December 15, 2024.

6. Resilience is further defined as flexibility and agility.

7. "Youth Not Attending School and Not Working by Age Group," The Annie E. Casey Foundation, accessed December 15, 2024.

8. *YouthBuild*, U.S. Department of Labor, accessed February 4, 2025.

9. "Youth and Work: Restoring Teen and Young Adult Connections to Opportunity, 2012," The Annie E. Casey Foundation, accessed December 15, 2024.

10. "Wage Tool," United for ALICE, accessed December 15, 2024.

11. "The Opportunity Passport: A Tool for Youth in Foster Care," The Annie E. Casey Foundation, 2009.

12. Orrell, Brent, and Hunter Dixon. *The Social Workplace: Social Capital, Human Dignity, and Work in America, Volume III,* American Enterprise Institute, 2024.

13. "Voice on the Job for Young Workers," UC San Diego, accessed February 4, 2025.

14. "CoLAB," Greater Washington Partnership, accessed December 15, 2024.

15. "X3 Internships," Future Focused Education, accessed December 15, 2024.

16. "X3 Mentor Frequently Asked Questions," Future Focused Education, accessed December 15, 2024.

17. Ibid.

18. These data comes from a non-public grant application submitted by X3 to the Casey Foundation.

19. "UNM Hospital Partnership to Increase Health Care Workers," University of New Mexico Health Sciences Center, last modified December 11, 2023.

20. Ibid.

21. "New Mexico Paid Intern Program Paves Professional Path for High School Student," NBC News, last modified December 2023.

22. "Our Principles," Partnership to Advance Youth Apprenticeship, New America, accessed December 15, 2024.

23. "Opening Doors for Young Parents," The Annie E. Casey Foundation, 2018.

24. Ibid.

25. "2023 KIDS COUNT Data Book," The Annie E. Casey Foundation, 2023.

26. "$122 Billion: The Growing, Annual Cost of the Infant-Toddler Child Care Crisis," National Conference of State Legislatures, 2023.

27. *2023 KIDS COUNT Data Book,* The Annie E. Casey Foundation, 2023.

Chapter 12: The Social Sector

1. "Charitable Giving Statistics," National Philanthropic Trust, accessed March 10, 2025.

2. "The Social Sector Infrastructure," Urban Institute, July 2023.

3. "The Tobacco Campaigns," Robert Wood Johnson Foundation, April 2011.

4. "8 Million Lives Saved Over 50 Years by Quitting Smoking, Study Finds," Fred Hutchinson Cancer Research Center, January 2014.

5. "History of the Nonprofit Sector Part 2: A (Very) Brief History of the U.S. Nonprofit Sector," Independent Sector, April 2019.

6. "How Many Nonprofits Are There in the US?" USAFacts, November 16, 2023.

7. "Downloadable Charts," Nonprofit Impact Matters, accessed December 15, 2024.

8. "Celebrating National Nonprofit Day with BLS Data," U.S. Bureau of Labor Statistics, August 17, 2023.

9. "Factsheet: The Importance of Out-of-School Time Programs," National Institute on Out-of-School Time, 2009.

10. Ibid.

11. "Fund Mapping 2023: Key Takeaways," Baltimore Promise, accessed December 15, 2024.

12. "Meet the YGs," Baltimore Promise, accessed December 15, 2024.

13. "Youth of the Year," Boys & Girls Clubs of America, accessed December 15, 2024.

Chapter 13: Coordination and Navigation

1. "The Urgent Need for Children's Cabinets," Usable Knowledge, Harvard Graduate School of Education, March 2020.

2. "Building and Empowering Impactful Children's Cabinets," National Governors Association, 2023.

3. Ibid.

4. "State Agency Child and Family Program Map," Indiana Department of Child Services, accessed December 15, 2024.

5. "Integrated Data Systems," The Annie E. Casey Foundation.

6. "The Game-Changing Potential of Data Integration in Transitioning Child Welfare," *Texas Tribune*, 2023.

7. "Co-Location of Services," Rural Health Information Hub, accessed December 15, 2024.

8. "Center for Working Families Framework: A Comprehensive Approach to Family Economic Security," The Annie E. Casey Foundation, 2020.

9. *The Center for Working Families Framework,* The Annie E. Casey Foundation, 2020.

10. Di Biase, Cori, and Marilia Mochel. *Navigators in Social Service Delivery Settings: A Review of the Literature with Relevance to Workforce Development Programs*, Manhattan Strategy Group, November 2, 2021.

11. *From Project to Platform: The Evolution of KIDS COUNT,* The Annie E. Casey Foundation, 2016.

12. "Home," StriveTogether, accessed December 16, 2024.

13. "Postsecondary Outcomes Story: Baltimore's Promise," StriveTogether, January 2023, accessed December 16, 2024.

Conclusion

1. Poon, Linda. "For Centuries, Peruvian Villagers Have Been Weaving This Grass Bridge by Hand," *National Geographic*, April 21, 2021.

2. Ibid.

3. Strohl, Jeff, Artem Gulish, and Catherine Morris. *The Future of Good Jobs: Projections Through 2031,* Georgetown University Center on Education and the Workforce, 2024.

4. Carnevale, Anthony P., Artem Gulish, and Kathryn Peltier Campbell. *If Not Now, When? The Urgent Need for an All-One-System Approach to Youth Policy.* Georgetown University Center on Education and the Workforce, 2021. Georgetown University Center on Education and the Workforce, 2021.

5. *Our Epidemic of Loneliness and Isolation: The Surgeon General's Advisory on the Healing Power of Social Connection,* U.S. Department of Health and Human Services, 2023.

6. Divecha, Diana. "How Teens Today Are Different from Past Generations," *Greater Good Magazine*, October 20, 2017.

7. Ibid.

Index

Abdul Latif Jameel Poverty Action Lab (J-PAL), 98
ACE. *See* adverse childhood experiences (ACE)
adolescence
   adult perspectives on adolescents, 11–12
   age range of adolescence, xx, xxi, 4, 11
   brain. *See* brains of adolescents
   challenges faced. *See* challenges adolescents face
   compassion we give toddlers, 11, 12, 26, 110
   as pivotal role in development, xiii, xx, xxiii
   family stability importance, 47, 122
   Federal Poverty Level, 52–54, 55
   five priority areas, xiii, xxi, 36–37. *See also* Thrive by 25 (Casey)
   importance of adult presence for adolescents, 21, 23, 60–63
   length of adolescence as uniquely human, 12, 191
   navigation guide through adolescence, 127–129
   puberty just one aspect of, 8
   puberty onset as beginning, xx, 4, 8
   thrills and peer opinions, xviii–xix, 11. *See also* risky behavior of adolescents

adoption or guardianship for, 66
   empathy practice for adolescent, 60, 62
   families, 21, 60–63, 122
   first jobs, 95–96, 100
   foster care improvement, 112–113
   juvenile justice system, 68, 113–114
   mentoring, 73–75
   partnerships between adults and teens, 110–112
   SOUL Family Legal Permanency, 66–67
adultification, 11
adverse childhood experiences (ACE), 18–21
   criminal justice system and, 27
   effects of constant adversity, 17
   presence of a trusted adult, 21, 23
   protective factors, 20–21
   those most affected, 25–30
   toxic stress, 21–23
   trauma, 23–25
Aidelemon, Esther, 89
Alaska Native Medical Center, 143
ALICE Essentials Index (Asset Limited, Income Constrained, Employed), 54–56
   Household Survival Budget, 55
   two-parent households, 55–56
The Annie E. Casey Foundation
   about, xiii, xiv–xv, 33–34
   adolescent brain science, xx, xxi, 35–36
   Brain Frames tool, xviii

Index

The Annie E. Casey Foundation (*cont.*)
  Center for Working Families, 181–182
  CEO Lisa Lawson, xiii, xiv–xv, xx, 29, 31, 33, 34, 37, 152
  core issues, 37
  drop-out prevention, 141
  ensuring youth reach their potential, xiii
  foster care, 34
  founded by Jim Casey and siblings, xvii, 30, 31, 33
  Generation Work, 100–101
  Jim Casey Initiative, 112–113
  Jim Casey Youth Opportunities Initiative, 156
  KIDS COUNT Data Book, 184–185
  Learn and Earn to Achieve Potential, 86–87, 145
  philanthropic organization, 166
  Pittsburgh Yards in Atlanta, 143–144
  predecessor presidents of, 195
  Team Decision Making, 146–147
  Thrive by 25. *See* Thrive by 25 (Casey)
apprenticeships, 96–97, 152–153
  Partnership to Advance Youth Apprenticeship, 161–162
  YouthBuild pre-apprenticeship program, 155, 160

Baez, Julia, 170
Baltimore's Promise collaborative, 170–171, 185
basic needs, 41–58
  about, 36, 37
  components of, 41–42, 45–51
  essential for success, xiii, xxi, 36, 41–42
  food, 45–46
  housing, 46–47
  importance of meeting, 41–42, 44, 57
  Maslow's Hierarchy of Needs, 43–44, 51
  mental and physical health, 47–49
  psychological needs, 51
  public benefits needed, 56, 123–124
  public service proactive approach, 139
  safety, 41, 49–50
  technology, 50–51
  unmet basic needs, 26, 51–57
  consequences of unmet basic needs, 51
belonging, 60, 126–127
Birmingham Children's Crusade, 115
birth rates for adolescents, 27
Boys & Girls Clubs of America, 173
  National Youth of the Year, 173
Brain Frames tool, xviii
brain stem, 8, 9
brains of adolescents
  adversity affecting, 16–18
  age range of adolescence, xx, xxi, 4, 11
  amygdala area, 106
  confinement in jail and, 68
  cortisol, 46
  development affected by trauma, 25
  development and caring adult, 62
  development back to front, 9, 10
  development in early childhood, 6–7
  development through adolescence, 7–8, 10–11, 26, 48, 51
  dopamine sensitivity, 11, 48, 51
  longing to be with family, 60
  neurons and synapses, 6, 10–11
  neuroplasticity of, 17
  positive experiences affecting, 17, 29
  poverty affecting, 56–57
  promise and potential of, 193
  pruning, 10–11

Index

structure of, 8–10, 9
trauma affecting, 25
weight at birth, 6
work and, 92–95, 153
Brewster, Jim, 31
bridge over Paiva River, 3–5, 187
  adolescence as bridge, 4–5, 13–14, 37, 187–188, 191
  obstacles on bridge to adulthood, 16. *See also* challenges adolescents face
Bronfenbrenner, Urie, 121

calls to action
  ecosystem for thriving, 131–132
  nonprofit organizations, 169–173
Cancel, Sixto, 59, 114
careers. *See* employers; financial stability; job training programs
caring connections. *See* permanent connections
Casey. *See* The Annie E. Casey Foundation
Casey, Jim
  challenges faced by youth, xxii, 34
  creating the Annie E. Casey Foundation, xvii, 30, 31, 33
  five priority areas for success, 36
  foster care focus, 34, 35
  founding UPS, xvii, xxii, 31
Center for Working Families (Casey), 181–182
Central New Mexico Community College program, 182
Centers for Disease Control and Prevention (CDC)
  adverse childhood experiences, 18, 19
  homicides among young people, 49
cerebellum, 9, 10
cerebrum, 9, 10
challenges adolescents face
  adverse childhood experiences, 18–21

adversity that is detrimental, 16–18
deep poverty, 26
economic uncertainty, 189
floor is lava, 15–16
foster care, 27–28
global challenges, 190
high school graduation, 80–81
individuals overcoming the odds, 28–30
juvenile justice system, 26–27
parenting as teens, 27. *See also* parenting as teens
positive youth development, 28
poverty, 26. *See also* poverty
presence of a trusted adult, 21, 23, 60–63
protective factors, 20–21
social fragmentation, 189–190
struggling but above poverty level, 54–56, 155
technological pressures, 188–189
those most affected, 25–30
toxic stress, 21–23
trauma, 23–25
child tax credit and poverty, 53
Child Welfare League of America, 34
child welfare systems, 63–67
  Connect program, 65–66
  cost of, 65
  families involved in decisions, 146
  first jobs and, 93
  foster care costs, 139. *See also* foster care
  high school graduation and, 81
  "lived expertise" wisdom, 140
  power to remove child from family, 63–65, 124, 138, 146
  removing child avoided via family assistance, 65, 138, 139–140, 146–147
  self-advocacy skill importance, 113
  sex trafficking and foster care, 67

Index

child welfare systems (*cont.*)
  SOUL Family Legal Permanency, 66–67
  Team Decision Making, 146–147
  Think of Us, 59
  Thriving Families, Safer Children, 140
childcare from employers, 162–163
  cost of insufficient childcare, 162
children's cabinets in government, 178–179
CNM Connect (Casey), 182
Coalition for Responsible Community Development, 86–87
Collaborative of Leaders in Academia and Business (CoLAB), 158
college
  CNM Connect helping students, 182
  complexity of transition to, 176
  food and college students, 45–46
  Generation Hope helping young parents, 78
  income and education, 79, 92
  persistence rates, 85–86
  student loan debt, 86
Connect program, 65–66
connections helping with challenges, 191. *See also* permanent connections
Consumer Price Index, 52
coordination among systems
  about need for, 175
  aligning efforts across systems, 184–186
  children's cabinets in government, 178–179
  data systems integrated, 179–181
  navigation, 182–184
  program eligibility integrated, 182
  putting the pieces together, 176–177, 179
  services integrated, 181–182
  Thrive by 25 areas of focus, 178

cortisol, 46
Costa Rica ecosystem, 119, 125–126
COVID-19 pandemic, 48, 50, 154
credentials. *See* education and credentials
criminal justice system. *See* juvenile justice system

Data Book on child well-being, 184–185
data systems integrated, 179–181
deep poverty, 26
depression, 48
development of the brain
  adversity affecting, 16–18
  amygdala activity, 106
  back to front, 9, 10
  caring adults and, 62
  confinement in jail and, 68
  development in early childhood, 6–7
  development through adolescence, 7–8, 10–11, 26, 48, 51
  executive function, 9, 10, 51
  information helpful to know, 13–14
  juvenile justice system ignoring, 26
  positive experiences affecting, 17, 29
  poverty affecting, 56–57
  pruning, 10–11
  trauma affecting, 25
disconnected youth, 100, 155–156
  Generation Work program, 100–101
  Strive Together initiative, 185
Dobrovolny, Delcie, 159
dopamine sensitivity, 11, 48, 51
Douglass, Frederick, vii, 127

East L.A. Walkouts, 115
Ecological Systems Theory (Bronfenbrenner), 121–122

Index

ecosystem for thriving, 119–133
  call to action, 131–132
  coordination among systems, 175.
    See also coordination among
    systems
  Costa Rica ecosystem, 119,
    125–126
  data systems integrated, 179–181
  description of ecosystems,
    119–120
  elements of adolescent ecosystem,
    122–125
  environment influencing
    development, 121–122
  failures of the ecosystem,
    124–125, 129–130
  family as heart of, 57, 122–123
  gaps and disorganization,
    129–130
  healthy relationships, 126–130
  navigating the ecosystem,
    127–129
  nonprofits, 124, 167
  protected ecosystem for growth, 120
  sectors with influence, 131–133.
    See also employers; government
    sector; nonprofits; philanthropy
  sense of belonging, 126–127
  strengthening the ecosystem,
    125–126
  unhealthy ecosystem, 130–131
  village to raise a child, 123, 125
education and credentials, 77–87
  about, 36
  benefits of, 78–79
  beyond high school, 85–87. *See
    also* college
  employment and education, 79, 92
  essential for success, xiii, xxi, 36
  flexible education models, 83–84
  Future Focused Education
    internships, 158–160
  Goodwill Excel Center, 84–85
  health needs affecting, 47–48
  housing instability and, 46

  Learn and Earn to Achieve
    Potential, 86–87
  motherhood and, 77–78
  traditional models not working, 82
  unemployment rate and, 79
  U.S. graduation rate, 81
empathy
  adolescent sensitivity, 60, 127
  leadership skills, 107
  practice with caring adults, 60, 62
Employer Signaling System (ESS;
  CoLAB), 158
employers
  about the private sector, 132
  adolescent brain and work, 92–95,
    153
  adolescent ecosystem, 124
  apprenticeships, 96–97, 152–153,
    161–162
  childcare for employees, 162–163
  disconnected youth reconnected,
    100–101, 155–156, 185
  examples of youth assistance
    programs, 158–162
  government sector regulations,
    136
  INROADS internship program,
    151–152
  job training programs. *See* job
    training programs
  paying living wages, 155, 157
  performing government sector
    work, 136
  role of, 153–154
  skill-building assistance for youth,
    157
  skills most in demand by, 154
  what young employees need,
    156–163
  work schedule instability, 157
employment. *See* employers; financial
  stability; job training programs
Esparza, Moctesuma, 115
executive function, 9, 10, 51
  "adulting," 177

Index

families
    adult presence for adolescent, 21, 60–63, 122
    Center for Working Families, 181–182
    child welfare systems, 63–67. *See also* child welfare systems; foster care
    Connect program, 65–66
    education prioritized, 77, 79
    family stability importance, 47, 122
    Generation Hope, 78
    government sector engaging families, 145–147
    heart of the adolescent ecosystem, 57, 122–123
    housing stability, 46, 47
    important roles of, 57
    juvenile justice system and, 67, 68–70, 146
    longing to belong to, 60, 126–127
    mitigating factors of trauma, 20–21
    neglect accusation risk, 47, 64
    poverty, 26, 37, 53, 65. *See also* poverty
    supporting, 37, 57, 65. *See also* The Annie E. Casey Foundation
    trauma from, 24
    two-parent households, 55–56. *See also* financial stability
Federal Poverty Level (FPL), 52–54, 155
    safety net programs, 53–54, 147
Felitti, Vincent, 18
financial literacy, 101–104, 182
financial stability, 89–104
    about, 36
    adolescent brain and work, 92–95, 153
    apprenticeships, 96–97, 152–153, 161–162
    benefits of teens working, 95–96
    economic uncertainty, 189
    education and employment, 79, 92
    employer in youth's ecosystem, 124. *See also* ecosystem for thriving; employers
    employment social enterprises, 99–101
    essential for success, xiii, xxi, 36, 89–90
    financial management and literacy, 101–104
    first paid job, 90–92, 152
    foster care exit help, 156
    Generation Work, 100–101
    Household Survival Budget, 55
    INROADS internship program, 151–152. *See also* job training programs
    IT training for better job, 89
    low-wage workers, 101–102
    percentage of young people employed, 91
    skills required for work, 94
    struggling but above poverty level, 54–56, 155
    summer jobs, 97–99
    two-parent households, 55–56
    youth employment programs, 98, 155
food as a basic need, 45–46
    school lunch programs, 141
Forum for Youth Investment, 126–127
foster care
    abuse experienced, 28, 59–60
    adolescent behavior leading to, 65
    adoption or guardianship, 66
    advocacy of Sixto Cancel, 59
    avoided via assisting families, 65, 138, 139–140, 146–147
    challenges faced by children, 27–28, 34
    child welfare systems, 63–67. *See also* child welfare systems
    costs of, 139
    disconnected youth reconnected, 155–156

financial help on exit, 156
first jobs and, 100
focusing on strengths not mistakes, 127
high school graduation challenges, 81
Jim Casey focusing on, 34, 35
Jim Casey Initiative, 112–113
Jim Casey Youth Opportunities Initiative, 156
kinship care, 66
LEAP education and employment, 86–87
"lived expertise" wisdom, 112
Opportunity Passport program, 156
poverty forcing children into, 47
sex trafficking and, 67
SOUL Family Legal Permanency, 66–67, 144–145
Think of Us, 59
Future Focused Education, 158–160

Galván, Adriana, 193
Gamble, Gwen Sanders, 115
Generation Hope, 78
Generation Work (Casey), 100–101
global challenges, 190
Goodwill Excel Center, 84–85
government sector
about, 132, 135–136
adolescents' power to influence, 148
children's cabinets, 178–179
cost-effective preventive approach, 139–141
data systems integrated, 179–181
disconnected youth reconnected, 155
enabling needed changes, 149
involving "customers," 141–145
involving families, 145–147
legislative and regulatory framework, 136
limited staff and funds, 136–137, 138
navigation aid, 182–184
policymaker importance, 147–149
prevention versus intervention, 137–141
public benefit money payoff, 139–140
reactionary policies, 138–139, 148
Team Decision Making approach, 146–147
UPS efficiency versus, 137
Grads2Careers (G2C), 185
graduation
challenge of, 80–81
drop-out prevention, 141
homeless student rates, 46
summer employment programs and, 98
U.S. high school rates, 81
growth of the brain. *See* development of the brain
gun violence, 41, 49
advocate Malala Yousafzai, 115
teen leader Naomi Wadler, 105–106
teens carrying guns, 49

Head Start, 121
health
adolescent brain and risky behaviors, 48, 51
as a basic need, 47–49
education and health, 79
screenings for health needs, 141
Hierarchy of Needs (Maslow), 43–44, 51
high school alternatives, 83–85
homelessness. *See* housing and homelessness
Hons, Amantha, 96–97
Hoopes, Stephanie, 54
Hope Center for College, Community, and Justice (Temple University), 45–46
Household Survival Budget, 55

Index

housing and homelessness
  affordable housing shortage, 47
  graduation rate and homelessness, 46
  housing as basic need, 46–47
  housing instability, 46, 47
  LEAP education and employment, 86–87
  number of homeless young adults, 46
  student turnover, 46–47
hunger, 45–46
  school lunch programs, 141

identity and sense of belonging, 127
incentive-based probation, 72–73
income and education, 79, 92
income and Grads2Careers, 185
Indiana's Commission on Improving the Status of Children, 179
INROADS internship program, 151–152
internet as a basic need, 50–51, 90
internships
  Future Focused Education, 158–160
  INROADS program, 151–152
  virtual internships, 154
  X3 internship program, 158–160

Jim Casey Initiative (Casey), 112–113
Jim Casey Youth Opportunities Initiative (Casey), 156
job training programs
  apprenticeships, 96–97, 152–153, 161–162
  Coalition for Responsible Community Development, 87
  education and employment, 79, 92. *See also* financial stability
  Employer Signaling System, 158
  Generation Work, 100–101
  government-funded summer jobs, 98
  Grads2Careers, 185

INROADS internship program, 151–152
  IT training for better job, 89
  matching to needed skills, 158
  New Moms, 99–100
  Partnership to Advance Youth Apprenticeship, 161–162
  Per Scholas, 89, 91
  skills most in demand, 154
  virtual internships, 154
  X3 internship program, 158–160
  YouthBuild, 155, 160
Johnson, Lyndon B., 52
juvenile justice system
  adversities of, 26–27
  changes via youth advocacy, 113–114
  disconnected youth reconnected, 155–156
  families and, 67, 68–70, 146
  first jobs and, 93, 100
  focusing on strengths not mistakes, 127
  high school graduation and, 81
  incentive-based probation, 72–73
  LEAP education and employment, 86–87
  permanent connections, 67–73
  probation, 70–73
  reactionary government policies, 148
  self-advocacy skill importance, 113–114
  summer employment programs and, 98

KIDS COUNT Data Book (Casey), 184–185
kinship care, 66

law enforcement. *See* juvenile justice system
Lawson, Lisa
  career with UPS, xiv, xvii, xxii, 31, 32–33, 34

Index

CEO of the Annie E. Casey Foundation, xiii, xiv–xv, xx, 29, 31, 37, 152
Leaders Organizing 2 Unite and Decriminalize (LOUD), 113–114
leadership opportunities, 105–116
  about, 36
  adolescents seeking advice and counsel, 111
  adult influences, 108–112, 115
  advocate Naomi Wadler, 105–106
  changemaker factors, 107
  decision-making about their lives, 110–111
  essential for success, xiii, xxi, 36
  movements led by young people, 115
  network of supportive relationships, 111–112
  self-advocacy, 107–108, 113–114
  self-development opportunities, 112
LEAP (Learn and Earn to Achieve Potential; Casey), 86–87, 145
  Coalition for Responsible Community Development, 86–87
Lewis, Nicole Lynn, 77–78, 114
lonesomeness epidemic, 189–190
LOUD (Leaders Organizing 2 Unite and Decriminalize), 113–114
low-wage workers, 101–102

Maslow, Abraham, 43–44, 51
McCarthy, Patrick, 195
Medicaid enrollees working full time, 56
mental health
  basic need, 48–49
  gun violence and, 41, 49
  homelessness effects, 46
  learning to manage emotions, 141
  self-advocacy strengthening, 107

mentoring, 73–75
  Future Focused Education, 158–160
  Generation Work program, 100–101
  INROADS internship program, 151–152
  Thread program, 74–75
money. *See* financial stability
Moore, Wes, xi–xvi, 135

narrative change work, 171
National Longitudinal Study of Adolescent to Adult Health, 47
navigation assistance with systems, 182–184
navigation through adolescence, 127–129
neglect, 64
  neglect accusation risk, 47, 64
  removing child from home, 64–65
Neighborhood Youth Corps, 155
Nelson, Doug, 195
neuroplasticity of the brain, 17
New Mexico Forum for Youth in Community, 113
New Moms, 99–100
nonprofits
  adolescent ecosystem, 124, 167
  adolescents co-designing programming, 170
  Alaska Native Medical Center, 143
  call to action, 169–173
  children's cabinets, 178–179
  donations and volunteers, 165
  examples of, 165
  Forum for Youth Investment, 126
  functions of, 124, 167
  Future Focused Education, 158–160
  Generation Hope, 78
  government sector regulations, 136
  history and growth of, 166–167

Index

nonprofits (*cont.*)
  navigation assistance, 182–184
  New Mexico Forum for Youth in Community, 113
  New Moms, 99–100
  Per Scholas, 89, 91
  performing government sector work, 136
  philanthropy supporting, 174
  positive narrative on youth, 171–173
  programming tailored to adolescents, 169–170
  resources for adolescents, 167–169
  social sector of influence, 132, 165–167
  summer job programs, 97–99
  tax-exempt status, 165
  Think of Us, 59
  Youth Grantmakers, 170–171

Opportunity Passport program (Casey), 156
Opportunity-Based Probation, 72–73
The Other Wes Moore (Gov. Moore), 135

parenting as teens, 27
  childcare from employers, 162–163
  education while, 77–78
  Generation Hope for college aid, 78
  New Moms supporting employment, 99–100
  Partnership to Advance Youth Apprenticeship (PAYA), 161–162
peer focus of adolescents, xviii–xix, 11
  self-advocacy importance, 108
  sexual activity, 48
Per Scholas, 89, 91
permanent connections, 59–75
  about, 36
  adoption or guardianship for, 66

  adult presence for adolescent, 21, 23, 60–63
  building healthy relationships, 126–130
  child welfare systems, 63–67
  essential for success, xiii, xxi, 36
  foster care versus family, 59–60, 65–66
  juvenile justice system and, 67–73
  Maslow's Hierarchy of Needs, 43–44, 51
  mentoring, 73–75
  SOUL Family Legal Permanency, 66–67
Perry, Bruce D., 20
philanthropy, 166, 173
  bringing together diverse stakeholders, 173, 174
  call to action, 173–174
  Casey as a philanthropic organization, 166
  power of, 166
  supporting nonprofits, 174
  UPS Foundation, xvii
physical health. *See* health
policymaker importance, 147–149. *See also* government sector
positive youth development approach, 28
  adolescent brains affected by, 17, 29
  Generation Work, 101
  mentoring, 73–75
  nonprofits' positive narratives, 171–173
poverty
  adversities of, 26
  affecting brain development, 17
  assisting family to avoid removing child, 65
  child tax credit and, 53
  college persistence rates, 85–86
  deep poverty, 26
  employment and education, 79, 92
  Federal Poverty Level, 52–54, 155

measuring, 52–53, 155
measuring via ALICE threshold, 55
neglect accusation risk, 47, 64
safety net programs, 53–54, 147
struggling but above poverty level, 54–56, 155
student turnover, 47
unmet basic needs, 52–57
prefrontal cortex, 9, 17
effects of constant adversity, 17
Pregnant Girl (Lewis), 78
private sector influence on adolescents, 132. *See also* employers
probation in juvenile justice system, 70–73
incentive-based probation, 72–73
pruning connections in the brain, 10–11
puberty
adolescence beginning with onset, xx, 4, 8
adolescence more than, 8
public systems. *See* government sector

Ramirez, David, 84–85
relationships, 126–130. *See also* permanent connections
risky behavior of adolescents
brain development, xviii–xix, 11
dopamine sensitivity, 11, 48, 51
education and, 79
juvenile justice system and, 26
probation and, 70–73
Robert Wood Johnson Foundation, 166
Ryan, Claude, 31

safety as a basic need, 49–50
gun violence, 41, 49
safety net programs, 53–54, 147
self-actualization, 43–44

self-advocacy
juvenile justice changes, 113–114
leadership and, 107–108, 113
sense of belonging, 60, 126–127
sex trafficking and foster care, 67
Sillas, Alli, 160
SNAP enrollees working full time, 56
social sector, 132, 165–167. *See also* nonprofits; philanthropy
Social Security Administration poverty thresholds, 52
social services versus UPS, 34–35, 37
SOUL Family Legal Permanency (Support, Opportunity, Unity, Legal relationships), 66–67, 144–145
Stand By Me NexGen, 102–103
Stillman, David, 180
stress
adult interaction for healthy response, 22
brain affected by, 46, 56–57
cortisol, 46
fight-or-flight mode from violence, 50
housing instability, 46
normal stress, 22
poverty causing, 56–57
tolerable stress, 22
toxic stress, 21–23
Strive Together initiative, 185
struggling but above poverty level, 54–56, 155
ALICE Essentials Index, 54–56
suicide, 48
summer jobs, 97–99
Supreme Court on adolescent justice, 72

Tackett, Jennifer, 107
tax-exempt status, 165
Team Decision Making (TDM; Casey), 146–147

Index

technology as a basic need, 50–51, 90
technology as a challenge, 188–189
teen parents, 27. *See also* parenting as teens
Temple University's Hope Center for College, Community, and Justice, 45–46
Think of Us, 59
Thread mentoring program, 74–75
Thrive by 25 (Casey)
  about, xiv, xxi, 194
  basic needs, 41–58
  collaboration among services, 178
  employers intersecting with, 153–154
  framework of essential needs, xiii, xxi, 36–37
  outcome objective, 41
  protective factors, 20
thriving, 191
Thriving Families, Safer Children initiative, 140
Thunberg, Greta, 115
Timons, Roszetta, 27
toddlers, 6–7
  adolescents needing same compassion, 11, 12, 26, 110
toxic stress, 21–23, 26, 56
trauma faced by youth, 23–25
  foster care, 28
  gun violence, 41
  juvenile justice system, 27
  self-advocacy skills, 113

UCLA Center for the Developing Adolescent, 193
unemployment rate
  education and, 79
  race and, 100
  youth versus adults, 100
United Parcel Service, 31. *See also* UPS
U.S. Census Bureau measuring poverty, 52
U.S. Department of Agriculture economy food plan, 52
United Way of Delaware Stand By Me NexGen, 102–103
University of New Mexico Hospital, 160
UPS
  American Messenger Company, 31
  children and family services versus, 34–35, 37
  founder Jim Casey, xvii, xxii, 31
  government processes versus, 137
  INROADS mentor, 151–152
  Lawson working for, xiv, xvii, xxii, 31, 32–33, 34
  success rate, 137
UPS Foundation, xvii

village to raise a child, 123, 125
virtual internships, 154

Wadler, Naomi, 105
work. *See* employers; financial stability; job training programs

X3 internship program, 158–160

Yousafzai, Malala, 115
Youth Development Study on work, 93
youth employment programs, 98, 155
Youth Grantmakers, 170–171
youth leadership. *See* leadership opportunities
YouthBuild pre-apprenticeship program (U.S. Department of Labor), 155
YouthBuild Philadelphia, 160

About the Author

Lisa M. Lawson is the president and chief executive officer of the Annie E. Casey Foundation. Since taking the helm in 2019, Lawson has spearheaded Casey's Thrive by 25 effort, which aims to improve outcomes for adolescents ages fourteen to twenty-four to ensure they successfully transition to adulthood. In 2023, she was selected as one of *Inside Philanthropy*'s fifty most powerful women in U.S. philanthropy. She lives in Baltimore.

Publishing in the Public Interest

Thank you for reading this book published by The New Press; we hope you enjoyed it. New Press books and authors play a crucial role in sparking conversations about the key political and social issues of our day.

We hope that you will stay in touch with us. Here are a few ways to keep up to date with our books, events, and the issues we cover:

- Sign up at www.thenewpress.com/subscribe to receive updates on New Press authors and issues and to be notified about local events
- www.facebook.com/newpressbooks
- www.twitter.com/thenewpress
- www.instagram.com/thenewpress

Please consider buying New Press books not only for yourself, but also for friends and family and to donate to schools, libraries, community centers, prison libraries, and other organizations involved with the issues our authors write about.

The New Press is a 501(c)(3) nonprofit organization; if you wish to support our work with a tax-deductible gift please visit www.thenewpress.com/donate or use the QR code below.